C000170704

This book by my long-standing [...]
markable. In a world of increas [...]
of how to find hope in the mid [...]
that we all face either now or [...]
pain and with real honesty Goff [...]
that a faithful God promises when we genuinely face life in all
its forms. If you really want to know hope as a reality then this
book will show you how. We will then have the wonderful opportunity to display that hope to all who long to know it too.
A book to read and then to put into practice!

David Holden, leader of New Ground churches,
part of Newfrontiers

Drawing from deep personal experience, Goff shares a moving epistle of the reality of pain and our powerful Christian
hope. This thoughtful, scriptural, heartfelt tour de force will
encourage you with God's amazing mercy and grace – now and
forever.

A must-read, whether you or someone you know is in the
midst of suffering or in readiness for a time of trial that may lie
up ahead for you. As you journey with Goff through this book
your faith and confidence in our great and loving God will be
strengthened and your soul comforted.

Lyndon Bowring, founder and chairman of CARE

I first met Goff Hope when I was a young man just starting
out in church leadership in Norwich. Goff was a kind and wise
guide, as full of encouragement as he was of faith. In this truly
splendid book, he shows that he is as helpful a guide now as
he was then. Writing from the fires of immensely challenging
personal experience, he shows from the Scriptures and from a
wide variety of Christian writings how faith in Christ can give

authentic hope, and be sustained even within times of terrible suffering. Goff writes beautifully, with profound pastoral empathy and with robust but approachable biblical faith. I cannot commend this book highly enough.

Revd Dr John Valentine, dean of the Local Ministry
Programme in the Anglican Diocese of Guildford,
church planter, theologian and trainer

Goff's life story is undeniable evidence that hope does, in fact, win. The book is filled with nuggets of pure gold truth that have been proven and tested in the most difficult circumstances that life can deal out to us. These nuggets hit on the root causes of hopelessness in the world today and destroy them. This is a good book. One that you will read through and then keep it close on your shelf as a reference to be referred to often.

Byron Brenneman, chairman of New Day Creations

Goff Hope is aptly named. In the midst of sickness and bereavement, he has discovered hope for every sufferer. If you have ever wondered where God is in the midst of your own suffering, or if you have ever wanted to offer real and solid comfort to a friend, then this is the book for you.

Phil Moore, author, pastor, speaker

Throughout this book, you will both laugh and cry, because it's a very earthy book written by a very humane man. But my guess is that once you've finished it, the sure and certain Christian hope will live in your heart more brightly than it did before you started. Read, laugh, cry, hope.

Stef Liston, church leader, author, training director and a leader
of Relational Mission, Newfrontiers

The world we live in tries to 'airbrush' life. Persuading us that happiness and fulfilment lie within reach through human effort or attitude, or by drawing from the many pleasures and pursuits we are told will bring us fulfilment. What happens, however, when the airbrushing wears off? When difficulty hits? When seemingly nothing and no one can fix things?

The pages of this book are written with raw honesty, touching on the realities that at some stage every human being must face. They are also written with wisdom, insight, application and above all centred on the perspective of Christian 'Hope'. This 'Hope' really is a gamechanger for every person on the planet. It shines brightly without the need for any airbrushing! Explore as you read. This will do you good.

Mike Betts, author, founder of Relational Mission churches

Hope Wins

How a vision of our eternal future impacts our lives today

Goff Hope

Authentic

First published 2023 by Authentic Media Limited,
PO Box 6326, Bletchley, Milton Keynes, MK1 9GG.
authenticmedia.co.uk

British Library Cataloguing in Publication Data
A catalogue record for this book is available from the British Library.
ISBN: 978-1-78893-276-9
978-1-78893-277-6 (e-book)

Cover design by Jennifer Burrell
Printed and bound by Bell and Bain Ltd, Glasgow

Contents

A Word of Thanks

This book would be quite incomplete without an expression of thanks to a number of dear friends who have played a significant part in our journey and without whose love, support and encouragement our story could have been very different.

We are grateful to God for Lyndon and Celia Bowring who, more years ago than I care to remember, were pivotal in our journey. Lyndon, I still remember you preaching a series on the book of Micah in those Kensington Temple days. I had never heard anything quite like it and it won me to the value of expository preaching. You took risks with me, inviting me to preach at KT, and were a big part of God's calling me away from a career at the BBC and off to London Bible College and pastoral ministry. Thank you.

Then there are our dear friends in the Newfrontiers family of churches, more names than I have space to mention, who really have been like family to us. Dave and Liz Holden – Dave I remember you from those Bible college days and am blessed to count you and Liz as valued friends over many years. Ray and Sue Lowe, Mike and Sue Betts, Stef and Davina Liston, Maurice and Rachel Nightingale and many more precious friends whose love and friendship we have valued and enjoyed, especially through the tough times – thank you. Terry, I can hardly begin to put into words how grateful we are to God for your fatherly leadership, godly example and prayerful support over many years. Like so many, we have benefitted hugely and been shaped by your life and ministry. Thank you.

Thank you too, those of you who have encouraged me in the writing of this book. Byron, you in particular have never wavered since those Beijing days in the belief that there was something to be written about our journey and have been such an inspiration and provocation. Authentic Media have of course played a very significant part in this project, believing in the idea of the book and giving me the opportunity to write. A special thank you to Claire Gough for patiently steering me through the process – your encouragement, kindness and hard work throughout have drawn it all together, made sense of my ideas and allowed me to express myself on some challenging themes.

Coming closer to home, Angie and I are so thankful to have had such a loving, supportive church family as King's Community Church here in Norwich, for over 30 years now. What a journey we have been on together! And what a blessing many of you have been to us personally through the good times and the difficult days of illness and great sadness. Thank you, precious church family.

Speaking of family, the last word of thanks surely goes to them; to Steve and Natalie whose attentive love and kindness through the darkest times has been priceless. You have watched for us, comforted us, encouraged and fed us when you yourselves were feeling the loss of dear Ali, and our wonderful grandchildren Thea and Jesse have brought much needed smiles and laughter throughout. We love you dearly, as we do you dear Dan, such a special son-in-law. We really didn't expect to walk such a painful path together but thank you for being such a loving, caring husband to Ali and brilliant dad to Annabelle and Luke.

Angie, everyone who knows you knows just how special you are, and none more than me. You are so thoughtful, loving and caring of others, often at a cost to yourself. What an adventure we have had together these past five decades, that has taken us from where we first met in London to different locations around the UK, and further afield. A journey in which, as well as sadness and tears, we have known God's rich blessing and deep sense of hope rooted in his gracious calling on our lives. What a blessed man I am to have you as a travelling companion! Thank you my love.

Foreword

You have in your hands a truly profound book, full of insights and lessons learned, often in great pain and pressure.

Having read it I feel like I have been taken by the hand into a glorious ancient building, and had doors opened to me into one breathtaking room after another. Light has been shed and truth has been uncovered. It has been an emotional rollercoaster.

This is no ordinary book. The subject of Hope certainly needs to be rediscovered by most of us. We tend to live for today, have expectations of fulfilment in this life and we live in a culture increasingly preoccupied with its rights and demanding those rights now. Some fight with increasing venom. Others yield to a prevailing cynicism and hopelessness that cripples many and robs them of any aspiration or optimism for the future.

Hope as described in the Scripture is a foreign concept to our modern unbelieving culture and sadly its loss has been felt in much of our Christian world. We too tend to live for today while the Bible urges us to fix our hope completely on the grace to be brought to us at the revelation of Jesus Christ (1 Peter 1:13). We too are impatient for pleasure and fulfilment in the immediate. Shortcuts are sought, corners cut. Hope for the future doesn't play the part that Scripture insists it should. Goff's book is full of biblical truth, reminding us of this fundamental foundation for the Christian life.

Powerfully illustrated and full of insightful quotations, Goff's book takes you on a journey that will move you profoundly but also instruct you significantly. Read seriously I believe it should change your understanding of life and readjust the centre of gravity of your worldview. You will see things differently.

Goff and his wife Angie have been living a life full of heart wrenching challenges and turns in the road one could never have anticipated. We are invited alongside to feel the pain, but also to learn the very precious and life changing lessons they have learned. We are taken with them into very dark places of distress, loss and agony but also into extraordinary heights of revelation that provide answers and hope.

Christians are not Stoics, pretending we feel no pain and enduring pressures with a British stiff upper lip. But neither are we sentimentally absorbed with our personal hurts and disappointments. Our journey is tough and for some very tough, but Christians are fortified by fellowship with one who was crucified in weakness but lives by the power of God.

We know a Saviour who for the joy set before him endured the cross, despising the shame. He invites us to follow him, fellowship with him and keep our eyes focused on the prospect of one day seeing him face-to-face, when all hope will be realized, fears be removed, tears wiped away and total joy be experienced.

This promised hope should garrison our hearts and fortify our minds for the journey. But ignoring this vital ingredient in our Christian life makes us vulnerable and defenceless, easily crushed by unexpected events, bewildered by dark clouds we might encounter.

New Testament believers were often converted into immediate persecution and pressure. To become a Christian was to embrace suffering and uncertainty. Their eternal hope provided the security they needed. It was more than enough to strengthen them and provide the joy that would equip them for all they would encounter.

We too must rediscover its vital role, benefit from Goff's wonderful book and adjust our perspective.

Terry Virgo, founder of Newfrontiers

Affectionately dedicated to our very dear daughter Ali.
Much loved and much missed.
One day, no more tears.
One day, all things new.
One day, what a reunion!
One day, face to face.

'Blessed is the one you choose and bring near,
to dwell in your courts!
We will be satisfied with the goodness of your house'

Psalm 65:4, ESV

Introduction

This is a book about hope, something that is in short supply in our times. In the English language hope is rather a small, ordinary, unimpressive little word that sounds nowhere near as exciting as other words carrying similar meaning, such as *aspiration*, *expectation*, or *yearning*, and yet it is a word that is fundamental to our happiness and wellbeing. Hope has the ability to excite, to lift our spirits. It has power to inspire great achievements, to endure hardship, press on in the face of incredible odds and remain resilient in desperate times. But should this little word be absent and our lives become hope-less it is possible for our whole demeanour to change, our energy be sapped and we can even lose the will to live. Such is the importance of hope.

Maybe you know what it is like to feel without hope, to have your hopes crushed. Maybe there are times when you hardly dare to ponder your future or the future of the world around you for fear of becoming overwhelmed. Or maybe, even if you're a Christian, you don't really know what the Bible says about the future and so rarely think about it. Sometimes it takes difficult circumstances to wake us up to the bigger questions of life, such as our future hope. Author Christopher Ash makes the point that there are two ways of asking hard questions: 'We may ask them as armchair questions or we may ask them as wheelchair questions.'[1] Two experiences that my wife,

Angie, and I have walked through in recent years have meant that this book is written very much from the latter standpoint.

In writing this book and telling our story I aim to show how fundamentally important hope is for human wellbeing, unmask the way fear works in our culture, and open up the magnificent future hope of the Christian message in a way that will, by God's grace, transform our lives. I am convinced that as Christians today we need to rediscover the importance of that clear and certain hope, what it means for us individually and for the world in which we live. Only then will we have the antidote to the epidemic of anxious fear that is in contemporary culture, rediscover 'inexpressible and glorious joy'[2] in the face of life's challenges, and have a message of astonishing hope for an increasingly hope-less generation.

> May the God of hope fill you with all joy and peace as you trust in him, so that you may overflow with hope by the power of the Holy Spirit.
>
> *Rom. 15:13*

1

Hope on Trial

Help, GOD – the bottom has fallen out of my life!
Master, hear my cry for help!
Listen hard! Open your ears!
Listen to my cries for mercy.

Ps. 130:1–2, MSG

You never forget the moment you hear the words, 'You probably already guessed – you have cancer.' Amazingly, I hadn't. My mind was racing, trying to process the shock-inducing news that I had stage 3 prostate cancer. I was a fit and, so I thought, healthy 56-year-old who took pride in my fitness, enjoyed running several times a week and rarely visited the doctors. Over the previous year or so I had experienced some minor health issues but nothing serious enough to slow me down or stop me running. I had gone to the doctor on the insistence of my wife, Angie. The results of a precautionary blood test suddenly set things in motion, but still I remained confident that nothing was seriously wrong. It was not until a few days later at an appointment with a consultant that I heard the words I will not forget in a hurry – 'you probably already guessed – you have cancer'. Suddenly my brain was whirring, trying to catch up with what the consultant had just said.

Among the carefully chosen words that medics use in these moments, the human brain has an uncanny knack of latching onto the one or two fear-inducing words. In my case it was 'cancer . . . haven't caught it early . . . aggressive . . . months . . .' Although I was actually being told that I didn't have just months to live but hopefully longer, it was the word 'months' that buried itself into my memory. I drove home with Angie in shocked silence. I couldn't think of anything to say. Suddenly all the things that just a few moments ago had been preoccupying my thoughts and had seemed so important, counted for little. My mind was in free-fall as I tried in vain to grasp all the competing implications of what I had just been told. I remember the following day, alone at home, crying out to God for his help: 'Lord, I don't know how to do this! Please help me, heal me!' I was not ready to die.

Born in coronation year, 1953, and growing up in London in the 1960s and 70s, like many others of my generation I never knew the horrors and hardships of war that our parents lived through. This was the affluent, swinging sixties with the promise of a bright future. I can remember exactly where I was at some historic moments, such as that Sunday night, 20 July 1969 when Neil Armstrong and Buzz Aldrin landed on the moon, making giant leaps for humankind. Then there was that Saturday afternoon, 30 July 1966 when England won the World Cup! Heady days indeed, full of promise. A few years earlier the then Prime Minister, Harold Macmillan, famously told the British public that they had never had it so good. Certainly, growing up in that era, even though there was war, suffering and poverty in faraway places, in the West many of us could expect a bright, happy future – healthy too, as medical science was making giant steps with the first heart transplant operations taking place around that time.

It is hard to believe now that the Humanist Manifesto II, written in 1973, although admitting that the first manifesto of 1933 had been overoptimistic, nevertheless retained the expectation that war would become obsolete and poverty would be eliminated. As for my personal hopes, although I had become a Christian in my teenage years after hearing Billy Graham preach, my hopes for the future were pretty much focused on this world with the aim of having an exciting career, falling in love with a wonderful girl and enjoying a comfortable, successful life. Although my dad died quite suddenly when I was in my early twenties, I had otherwise little personal experience of bereavement and thoughts about death just did not figure in my thinking. Any contemplation of heaven was somewhat wispy, involving angels and streets of gold, all of which, if I am honest, was not particularly appealing. By the early 1970s I had a dream job, working for the BBC at the studios in London, at a time when *Top of the Pops*, *Monty Python's Flying Circus* and many other now classic programmes were being made – and I was being paid to work there! Conveniently, I was often working irregular hours which gave me the perfect excuse for missing church on Sundays, no questions asked.

Around that time, I visited a church in London that I immediately recognized as being different. Instead of the rather dull formalism that I was used to (believe me, in the 1970s it was considered daring, even worldly, to have a guitar in church), here there were people singing, worshipping God with obvious joy and enthusiasm. It wasn't that I was a seeker on a spiritual journey, trying to find a deeper meaning to my faith; if the truth be known, my only reason for going was to meet a girl who I knew went there. But here I was, a Christian who had made a decision to follow Christ, and yet spending most days feeling a little guilty that I wasn't quite what I ought to be. I was faced with people of all ages who, unlike me, did not seem to be embarrassed about their faith but rather joyfully sang and spoke of Jesus as someone they knew, loved and lived for.

As the weeks went by, I began to hear about the Holy Spirit, something that I had not heard talked about very much before. I learned of the promise that Jesus made to his disciples before he left them and ascended to heaven, how he would not leave them to live the Christian life in their own strength, but that he would send the Holy Spirit, the Comforter, who would come and be with them, encouraging them in Jesus' absence. Not only that, but he would also empower them, giving them boldness and joy for the journey by making Jesus real to them. And this promise, I discovered, was for us too! There it was in the Bible!

I remember thinking that if this was true, that we could be filled with boldness, be helped in our praying, and know the joy-giving presence of the Lord in our daily lives, why on earth would we not want it? I knew only too well the reality gap in my own life between what I believed and how I lived, and so set about discovering this for myself. I returned week after week, hungrily asking God to give me what I saw these people had, to fill my life with the Holy Spirit just as Jesus promised his disciples.[1] Theologian and writer J.I. Packer, in his book *Keep in Step with the Spirit*, likens the Holy Spirit's role in our lives to that of floodlights, illuminating for us what is otherwise obscured and not at all clear to see.[2] If you have ever been at a football match when the floodlights suddenly go out, you will know that the game just has to stop. You are in the dark and can't see properly. But as soon as the lights come on again, up goes a cheer because all becomes clear. You can see the action. You are no longer in the dark. So too with the Holy Spirit; he throws the floodlights on Jesus, making him wonderfully real to us.

I remember so clearly the evening, now more than forty years ago, when God answered my prayer and the Holy Spirit filled me to overflowing as he threw the floodlights on Jesus, making him real, personal and present with me in such a way that I could not be a nominal, half-hearted Christian any longer. I will say more about this later in the book, but enough to say at this point that it would lead me in the years that followed to leave my career in television to study theology, before becoming a pastor and church leader. I had met my future wife, Angie, at this time and asked her if she would marry me with the not very reassuring words: 'I am about to resign my job and go to Bible college for three years because I believe God wants me to get prepared for an adventure ahead, so if you are up for this adventure with me, will you marry me?' Thankfully she said yes! And what an adventure it has been, knowing the leading and goodness of God over the years. Not always easy but always rewarding. One of the biggest adventures was setting out for Norwich, more than thirty years ago, with our young family, not quite knowing how life would work out but believing that God was calling us to come and serve a church family here.

In the years that followed, like any other Christians, we had our challenges that drove us to our knees, and our blessings that made us gratefully aware of God's gracious care for us. God was very good to us, giving us a beautiful family, a son and a daughter, Steve and Alison, who were a delight and joy, both becoming Christians at a young age and set on living their lives as followers of Jesus. Yes, we had our ups and downs over the years but coming into our fifties we were able to look back and say that God had been good to us. We were blessed.

And then cancer struck. Here I was, still at least ten years away from planned retirement, facing the real prospect of

dying what I considered to be a premature death. That was
not in the script. The truth is, we tend to think that we are in
control of much of our lives, that we can expect to live a long
and relatively healthy life, thanks to medical science and the
comforts of our modern, affluent lifestyles. When our comfort
zones are rocked by something like cancer, however, we realize
that in fact we are really rather frail. Being a Christian doesn't
change that. One of the wonderful things about the book of
Psalms is that the psalmist gives expression to all the experiences and emotions of life to God, and encourages us to do
likewise. David, who wrote many of the psalms, was known for
his music, for his song of praise (in fact in one place he is called
'Israel's beloved singer of songs'[3]) but he also knew how to pour
out his heart to God – very graphically – when faced with painful and trying situations. The words quoted at the start of this
chapter echo how I felt in those moments after my diagnosis:

> Help, GOD – the bottom has fallen out of my life!
> Master, hear my cry for help!
> Listen hard! Open your ears!
> Listen to my cries for mercy.

In the days, weeks and months that followed, I learned some
important lessons about the nature of fear and faith, the way
we think, and the importance of having a solid, living, future
hope. As a Christian of many years, I of course had the wonderful assurance that I belonged to Jesus, that I was loved with
an everlasting love and that one day I would go to be with him,
awaiting the day when he will make all things new. I knew
these things. I had even taught on the subject of eschatology,
the book of Revelation, and our future hope, for many years.
But in the weeks that followed that diagnosis I learned very

quickly that my hope needed to be clearer and closer to hand. It had to be a daily, ongoing reality if I wasn't to slip into anxious, fear-filled thoughts. I realized too how easy it is to live in a version of Christianity that is long on the here and now, and short on the yet to come, especially when living in the relative comfort and security of the West, with little threat of physical persecution and every expectation of a long, fulfilled life. We are prone to forget that in the history and experience of the church worldwide, our relative ease and comfort as Christians is quite unusual. Certainly for the first 300 years of the church's history, suffering and martyrdom was commonplace for Christians, and in many parts of the world today that remains the case.

Of course, it is a blessing to be able to live our lives in peace and plenty, and we are grateful to God for it and pray for peace across the nations for the sake of the gospel. However, it does open up the very real possibility of settling, of putting our roots down and thinking of this life as though it is the main act when, of course, for the Christian it is merely the prelude – not to be confused with or exchanged for the magnificent future hope to be revealed when Jesus returns and raises the curtain on his new creation.

2

When Hope Dies

If you lose hope, somehow you lose the vitality that keeps life moving, you lose that courage to be, that quality that helps you go on in spite of it all. And so today I still have a dream.

Martin Luther King[1]

It is perhaps appropriate that I get to write a book about hope, given my name. I was brought up in a family where I was surrounded by hopes – my father's name was Ken Hope and believe it or not, he met a young woman by the name of Hope Cundy, so when they married she became Hope Hope! And then there were my three sisters. So it really is true to say that I grew up surrounded by Hopes.

Growing up in the days when we were addressed at school by our surnames, I remember the word (less fondly, it has to be said) being bellowed across the classroom when some sort of trouble was coming my way. Then the quips when being asked my name – 'hope springs eternal' and so on – to which I have learned to nod politely, feigning amusement, having heard it endless times. But then every now and again a more thoughtful person will respond with: 'What a great name . . . that is such a good word . . .' And they are right. Hope is a very good word. But it is a very nervous word in our culture. By that I mean that the way we use it usually expresses considerable uncertainty: 'I hope it won't rain tomorrow', 'I hope I pass my exams', 'I hope my money lasts till the end of the month', 'I hope there isn't a terrorist attack', 'I hope I will get better', 'I hope I will find happiness in life'. And the reason hope has become a nervous word is that we live in a culture that is very uncertain about the future.

Change is happening all around us, whether it be climate change, regime change, economic change. Every day we are bombarded with a constant outpouring of unprocessed news and information concerning up-to-the-minute happenings all around the world that threaten to change the status quo. There are the millions of migrants on the move trying to find somewhere in the world to call home, perhaps threatening our lifestyle, the latest terrorist attack, market downturn or health scare. To make matters worse, those who deal in news love to use words such as 'crisis', 'tragic', 'shock', 'fatal', 'scare', to prey on our fears and get our attention. And then there was Covid. You could say that fear is now of epidemic proportions. Since I wrote the above words Russia has invaded Ukraine, thousands have been killed, millions forced to flee their homes and there is the very real threat of the use of chemical weapons. Even the possibility of nuclear weapons being deployed has been in the news – and all this on our doorstep. Hope is in short supply.

It is one of the wonders of being a human being that we have the God-given capacity to imagine, anticipate, to long for, to hope, and when that is gone, life becomes very bleak. Just a spark of hope about something good and pleasant ahead can make such a difference; it lifts our spirits in the humdrum of life, puts a smile on our face and a skip back in our step. It energizes us. Children know all about this; it comes naturally to them – do you remember getting excited about Christmas and birthdays weeks or even months beforehand, eagerly ticking off the days? Today is a special day, it's my granddaughter's birthday, and when you are 6 years old that is very exciting! But her excitement didn't just start today – it began weeks ago when she was told that her birthday was approaching and she began imagining the day, dreaming of the presents that might be in store for her and getting excited at the prospect of a party ahead. She has been excitedly counting down the days in anticipation for weeks!

Of course, over the years we begin to discover that life can be disappointing as things don't always work out the way we had hoped. To this day I can remember as a child my parents on occasions warning me not to raise my hopes too much because it might lead to disappointment, and sure enough disappointments do come along to dampen our hopes. It is too easy to become cynical and dismiss excited anticipation as childish naiveté or youthful exuberance, and get robbed of a wonderful gift in the process. That is part of growing up; discovering the harsh reality that all is not well in the world, that people and things disappoint and don't live up to our expectations. And then there are the challenges of grief, loss and physical frailty that come knocking on our door, threatening to rob us of our joy and sense of expectation. If that wasn't enough, there is the sheer weight of living in an uncertain world where fear of some kind is always in the news and a topic of conversation. It is hardly surprising that the NHS prescribed a record number of antidepressants in 2016: 64.7 million items according to the most recent annual data from NHS, an all-time high.[2] That's about the same number as the population of the UK, and two years of COVID-19 have no doubt made those figures a lot worse.

I recently read a disturbing news article entitled 'Resignation Syndrome: Sweden's mystery illness'[3] describing a strange debilitating illness that, it would appear, only affects children of asylum seekers. Apparently, these otherwise healthy children just withdraw completely from normal life, ceasing to talk or walk or even open their eyes for months or even years. They seem no longer able to interact with the world around them or even to feed themselves. The children most vulnerable to 'Resignation Syndrome' are those who have been forced to flee their homes, often in violent circumstances, in search of somewhere safe to live. Some have been held in camps for long periods of time, moved from pillar to post waiting for a nation to receive them. At first it was suspected that they were faking illness in order to be given residency, but as the months and years have gone by it appears that these dear children just became overwhelmed with fear and hopelessness such that their bodies and minds shut down.

In his book *Man's Search for Meaning*, Viktor Frankl, a Jew in Nazi Germany who survived Auschwitz, wrote of his experience and that of his fellow prisoners. Before the war, Frankl had been a doctor and psychiatrist, trained to observe human behaviour. In the daily horrors of the prison camp, he observed:

The prisoner who had lost faith in the future – his future – was doomed. With his loss of belief in the future, he also lost his spiritual hold; he let himself decline and became subject to mental and physical decay. Usually this happened quite suddenly . . . Usually it began with the prisoner refusing one morning to get dressed and wash or to go out on the parade grounds. No entreaties, no blows, no threats had any effect. He just lay there, hardly moving. If this crisis was brought about by an illness, he refused to be taken to the sick-bay or to do anything to help himself. He simply gave up . . . When we spoke about attempts to give a man in camp mental courage, we said that he had to be shown something to look forward to in the future.[4]

As human beings, we need something in our future to be excited about, to be optimistic about, otherwise we are prone to discouragement and even depression. Made in God's image,[5] we have the capacity to dream dreams, to contemplate beautiful landscapes, to imagine wonderful settings and exciting possibilities. Like a mechanical clock or watch that relies on its mainspring to provide the energy to keep the cogs and wheels turning, so we need the impetus of hope to energize our lives. If it isn't there, if life becomes hopeless, then we begin to malfunction, our heads go down and all enthusiasm for life drains out. The reason we have this yearning, this capacity to hope, is that we were made with the capacity to know God, to comprehend something of the awesome majesty and beauty of the one who, with a word, brought all creation into being, fashioning the world with all its stunning panoramas and delicate designs, who threw stars into their orbits yet knows when one small bird falls to the ground. But having forfeited that relationship, we are left searching for anything big enough to fill the void, to live for, to dream of.

Martin Luther King, quoted at the beginning of this chapter, is most famously known for his speech 'I Have a Dream' which he delivered to 250,000 civil rights supporters, on the steps of the Lincoln Memorial in Washington in 1963. What you may not know is that four years earlier he preached a sermon at his home church in Montgomery, Alabama, entitled 'Shattered Dreams'. This was around the time of the Montgomery bus boycott when his home was attacked and he and others ended up in jail as a result of their protest against segregation and the treatment of African-Americans. In that sermon he spoke about hope and how easily it can be lost:

> One of the most agonising problems within our human experience is that few, if any, of us live to see our fondest hopes fulfilled.

The hopes of our childhood and the promises of our mature years are unfinished symphonies . . . Shattered dreams are a hallmark of our mortal life.

He went on to ask what our response as Christians should be to disappointments, ruling out bitterness and resentment, and concluding that we must:

⌐accept finite disappointment, but never lose infinite hope.⌐ Only in this way shall we live without the fatigue of bitterness and the drain of resentment . . . the Christian faith makes it possible for us notably to accept that which cannot be changed, to meet disappointments and sorrow with an inner poise, and to absorb the most intense pain without abandoning our sense of hope, for we know, as Paul testified, in life or in death, in Spain or in Rome, 'that all things work together for good to them that love God, to them who are called according to his purpose.'[6]

Martin Luther King understood the importance of holding on to hope in the face of difficulties if we are to avoid being drained of vitality and courage. His faith as a Christian and his confidence in God who had called him fuelled his hope, his dream, his vision of a world where freedom and justice reign. It was far from easy but he kept going, despite numerous disappointments. It would eventually lead to significant change in the nation, but it would cost him his life. On the 4 April 1968, just five years after his famous 'I Have a Dream' speech, he was assassinated. You can only live that kind of life when you have, in his words, an infinite hope, a hope that goes beyond the present.

Shattered dreams are indeed a hallmark of our mortal lives. We too face disappointments and setbacks that threaten to drain us of our hope and happiness. It might be a broken relationship, or a bereavement, an illness or fearful, unwelcome news. Being diagnosed with cancer certainly was for me an unwelcome shock that in the moment drained me of vitality and joy. It is as though in those moments when our dreams are shattered, our minds quickly search for something or someone to cling onto, something substantial enough and strong enough to stop us from sinking into gloomy hopelessness. In my case I remember receiving a number of emails from some well-intentioned individuals informing me of some weird and wonderful diets that were apparently known to cure cancer. I can't say I tried them, although the asparagus diet was certainly tempting! But those challenging moments are also moments of opportunity, because in that instant the trivial preoccupations of life that claim our efforts and hold our attention for most of the time, suddenly fall away, and we become more receptive to the discovery of the things that really matter.

Like the psalm quoted at the start of the last chapter, it is often a moment when we desperately cry out to God in prayer. Maybe you can identify with that, and know what it is like for your whole world to be turned upside down by an unexpected turn of events. Well, I would encourage you to keep reading because it is my intention to explore the magnificent hope of the Christian, to discover how we can cultivate this hope for the future such that our lives do not become gripped by fear in the face of bad news or difficult days.

3

Hope in the Face of Illness

*God whispers to us in our pleasures, speaks in our conscience, but
shouts in our pains: it is his megaphone to rouse a deaf world.*
C.S. Lewis[1]

Cancer has the ability to awaken us to the fact that we are finite
beings. It should be obvious to us all that we will all die, but
somehow we manage to bury that reality sufficiently so that it
comes as something of a shock to be told that we have a terminal illness. I had been told that because I had metastatic secondary growths, the cancer could not be removed and that the
best I could expect was a course of radiotherapy followed by
drugs to try to keep it under control. Of course, as Christians
we believe that we have been made in the image of God[2] and
that although our bodies are 'wasting away',[3] there is a part of
us that is eternal. Nevertheless, we too are shocked and fearful on hearing that our time on earth is limited, that death is
approaching.

This moment of shock is dangerous, because what often happens next is a series of 'what if' questions present themselves.
Think of the last time you were faced with some challenging
news or information – isn't that what happened? A series of
'what ifs' flooded your mind, and how creative they can be!

Maybe you did a quick google search to try to find out more, and that just led to more 'what ifs'. Unchecked they will explore no end of fear-filled options, passing them on to your imagination to fill out the details, and before you know where you are, your whole demeanour has changed, your joy has gone, and so has your enthusiasm. You have become discouraged. But then I began to hear another voice speaking to me.

A few days before I went to see that consultant to be told my diagnosis, I had wandered into a second-hand bookshop, something I rather like to do, and bought on impulse a little book by Henri Nouwen entitled *In the House of the Lord*. I say on impulse, but actually I believe it was the leading and kindness of my heavenly Father, because the day after I had been diagnosed I picked it up and read the following: '"Do not be afraid, have no fear", is the voice we most need to hear . . . Why is there no reason to fear any longer? Jesus himself answers this question succinctly when he approaches his frightened disciples walking on the lake: "It is I; do not be afraid" (John 6:10)'.[4]

In his little book, Henri Nouwen points out that we are a fearful people, surrounded by a culture that is full of fear, so much so it could be called a 'house of fear'. He then goes on to say that Jesus offers us an alternative; that he calls us into fellowship with himself, to abide in him, to live in the house of the Lord rather than the house of fear. What a wonderful invitation! That really struck me; the fact that I have a choice each day, each moment of the day, as to where I will live. Will I drift with the culture around me into the house of fear or will I make my home in the house of the Lord? He continues:

The agenda of our world – the issues and items that fill our newspapers and newscasts – is an agenda of fear and power. It is amazing, yes frightening, to see how easily that agenda becomes ours . . . Look at the many 'if' questions we raise: 'What am I going to do if I do not find a spouse, a house, a job, a friend, a benefactor? What am I going to do if they fire me, if I get sick, if an accident happens, if I lose my friends, if my marriage does not work out, if a war breaks out?

It was the following that really spoke into my heart: 'Fearful questions never lead to love-filled answers; underneath every fearful question many other fearful questions are hidden.'[5] Ponder for a moment. Once we start on the path of exploring the fear-filled possibilities, is it not the case that the process rarely results in our becoming peacefully happy? Usually a whole range of fear-inducing possibilities quickly present themselves, and we end up thoroughly discouraged. In the days following my diagnosis I quickly realized that if I opened the door to 'what if' questions, I could become discouraged, downhearted and then depressed in no time at all. Instead, I discovered more than ever before the need to come quickly into the presence of the Lord at the start of each day, to take hold of that life-changing invitation to live in the house of the Lord, enjoying the company of my Lord and Saviour, the birthright of every Christian, instead of drifting into the house of fear. John the disciple of Jesus wrote his Gospel somewhat differently to Matthew, Mark and Luke. Rather than just writing narrative, important though that is, he often chose to use rather more poetic language, drawing out themes to help us understand the unique and special events that he witnessed. One of those themes is 'abiding' or 'remaining', a word which he uses forty times in his Gospel. At the start of his own journey with Jesus, John uses that word three times:

Jesus turned and saw them following and said to them, 'What are you seeking?' And they said to him, 'Rabbi' (which means Teacher), 'where are you staying?' He said to them, 'Come and you will see.' So they came and saw where he was staying, and they stayed with him that day, for it was about the tenth hour.

John 1:38–39, ESV

The word in Greek is *meno*, which means to remain, stay in a place, so John's journey as a follower of Jesus began when he chose to remain, stay where Jesus was. Moving on to John chapter 15, in some of the best-known words of Jesus where he tells his disciples that he is the vine and they are like branches, Jesus uses the same word *meno*, stay / remain / abide, eleven times in just thirteen verses, to stress the importance of this vital connection with him. 'Stay close! Stay with me!' What a wonderful invitation!

Another unexpected moment came a day or two later. I was in my study, browsing through some books, trying to occupy my thoughts, when a small card dropped out of one of them. I picked it up and read the following words:

Do not be anxious about anything, but in every situation, by prayer and petition, with thanksgiving, present your requests to God. And the peace of God, which transcends all understanding, will guard your hearts and your minds in Christ Jesus. Finally, brothers and sisters, whatever is true, whatever is noble, whatever is right, whatever is pure, whatever is lovely, whatever is admirable – if anything is excellent or praiseworthy – think about such things.

Phil. 4:6–8

It had my grandfather's name on it, and on closer inspection I realized that it was a little card that he used when visiting his congregation more than fifty years ago. He was a vicar and had died shortly after I was born so I never knew him, but here he was passing onto me some wonderful, timely encouragement through a visiting card! In the days and weeks that followed I began to realize how important this battle for the mind is, on a moment-by-moment basis. I came to see that prior to this point in my life I had actually been quite careless in my thinking, sometimes allowing myself to entertain discouraging or worrying thoughts for a day or two, robbing me of God's peace, ruining my day and making me something of a misery to live with. What a fool I had been! I now came to see that every day is precious and not to be wasted. I was not going to be so careless now. So, on waking in the morning, realizing that my mind was keen to remind me of the cancer and the potential problems ahead, making me fearful and depressed in minutes, I came to see the importance of that moment. Rather than lying in bed allowing that to happen, I remembered that I had a wonderful alternative, a way of escape, and wasted no time in coming into the presence of the Lord, preferring by far the peace and joy to be found there to the misery and depression awaiting me in the company of fearful thoughts. In the words of the late J.I. Packer that I often bring to mind when I begin to flounder, questioning whether God is there and if he cares about me:

> The Bible is the rope God throws us in order to ensure that we stay connected while the rescue is in progress . . . To moderns drowning in hopelessness, disappointed, disillusioned, despairing, emotionally isolated, bitter and aching inside, Bible truth comes as a lifeline, for it is future-oriented and hope-centered throughout.[6]

It had been my practice for years to climb the steps to my study in the loft first thing in the morning to spend time alone with my heavenly Father, before other distractions of the day presented themselves. That routine now became more important than ever – literally a lifeline, reminding myself of God's goodness, his greatness, his grace – opening my Bible and holding onto those magnificent truths and promises and asking my heavenly Father to speak to me. It wasn't that I was being very pious; rather I was desperate, much preferring the presence of the Lord to the fears that my mind conjured up. In the words of Joni Eareckson Tada, who has endured more physical suffering than most of us will ever know, 'Suffering lobs a hand-grenade into our self-centredness, blasting our soul bare, so we can be better bonded to the Saviour.'[7] Facing me at the top of the stairs at the entrance to my loft is a picture of the sun rising over the earth, taken from the International Space Station, with the words of Dietrich Bonhoeffer inscribed underneath:

> At the threshold of the new day stands the Lord who made it. All the darkness and distraction of the dreams of night retreat before the clear light of Jesus Christ and his wakening Word. All unrest, all impurity, all care and anxiety flee before him. Therefore, at the beginning of the day let all distraction and empty talk be silenced and let the first thought and the first word belong to him to whom our whole life belongs.[8]

Those morning times have been so important for me. I remember early on in my life as a Christian thinking that this duty of daily devotions, or 'quiet times' as they used to be called, was a chore to be done, a box to be ticked in order to win God's approval, keep him on my side. But of course, with that kind of mindset far more attractive options presented themselves at the start of the day (such as staying in bed!) and so my 'devotions' were quite sporadic. However, as the years went by, I realized that the key to enjoying and benefiting from those times, the way to move from duty to delight, was to have my eyes opened to the way I am thought of by my Father God. This is absolutely crucial when it comes to our devotions, our prayer lives, and it was a turning point in my journey as a Christian when God spoke to me many years ago and opened my eyes to his outrageous, extravagant, gracious love for me. I was reading a book by J.I. Packer entitled *Knowing God*, and I came to a paragraph in the chapter 'Knowing and Being Known' and read the following. It is rather a long quote but well worth the reading:

What matters supremely, therefore, is not, in the last analysis, the fact that I know God, but the larger fact which underlies it – the fact that He knows me. I am graven on the palms of His hands. I am never out of His mind. All my knowledge of Him depends on His sustained initiative in knowing me. I know Him, because He first knew me, and continues to know me. He knows me as a friend, one who loves me; and there is no moment when His eye is off me, or His attention distracted from me, and no moment, therefore, when His care falters.

This is momentous knowledge. There is unspeakable comfort – the sort of comfort that energises, be it said, not enervates – in knowing that God is constantly taking knowledge of me in love, and watching over me for my good. There is tremendous relief in knowing that His love to me is utterly realistic, based at every point on prior knowledge of the worst about me, so that no discovery now can disillusion him about me, in the way I am so often disillusioned about myself, and quench His determination to bless me. There is, certainly, great cause for humility in the thought that He sees all the twisted things about me that my fellow-men do not see (and am I glad!), and that He sees more corruption in me than that which I see in myself (which, in all conscience, is enough). There is, however, equally great incentive to worship and love God in the thought that, for some unfathomable reason, He wants me as His friend, and desires to be my friend, and has given His Son to die for me in order to realize this purpose.[9]

What astonishing truth! I first read those words more than thirty years ago and pretty much committed them to memory, going back to them again and again. It has become my favourite quote outside the Bible. Why? Because I constantly need to be reminded of God's amazing grace and how it has transformed the way he thinks of me – forever! What a difference it makes to know that God doesn't just tolerate you, but likes you! More than that, he loves you with a love that it will take you an eternity to fully comprehend. How different those morning moments become when you realize that you are coming to someone who views you in this way and welcomes you into his presence enthusiastically. How important after my cancer diagnosis, at a moment when I could have been tempted to think that God had abandoned me and didn't care about me or my condition.

This is such an important subject that I will continue in the following chapter to explore more fully the relationship that God desires to have with us and how he is able to use those painful experiences in our lives to bring it about.

4

Hope in the Face of a Father

*'Abba.' Small as this word is, it says ever so much. It says: 'My
Father, I am in great trouble and you seem so far away. But I know
I am your child, because you are my Father for Christ's sake. I am
loved by you because of the Beloved.'*

Martin Luther[1]

In the early days after my diagnosis, I was tempted to turn
to my laptop to google 'prostate cancer' in an attempt to understand a little more about the condition and what might lie
ahead. I quickly discovered that this was not a good place to
turn, as it only fuelled my fears as I read about the various
symptoms, stages and outcomes that I might expect.

Little children know where to turn when they get hurt or
become frightened. They run to someone whose love and care
is guaranteed – a parent, a mum, a dad. The word *abba* in the
quote above is an Aramaic word meaning 'father', but more like
our informal or childish expression 'dada' or 'papa' in English –
one of the first words that a child manages to say, much to the
delight of the parents! Martin Luther, after years of seeking
to win God's approval through rigorous religious practice, had
discovered the childlike joy of knowing God as his Father to

whom he could turn in any crisis or moment of need – and he faced many!

The first and most important step in escaping the fear, insecurity and hopelessness that a life-threatening illness such as cancer can bring is to know that you are not alone, that your future is not in the hands of chance, or even in the hands of medics, although we do of course value highly their skills and dedication. When you begin to understand and grasp the fact that as a Christian you not only have a future that goes beyond the grave, but you also have God as your Father, watching and caring for you better than any earthly father, committed to your good and to bringing you home to himself one day, it changes everything. And that is true for every Christian. I have a playlist of hymns and worship songs on my phone that I use just about every day to encourage my heart and drive out anxious fear in challenging moments. In the days following my diagnosis I came across a song written by Matt Redman entitled 'The Father's Song' that became a favourite and a source of great reassurance at that time. The lyrics carry beautiful Biblical truth about God's Father heart towards every believer:

> Heaven's perfect melody, the Creator's symphony
> You are singing over me, the Father's song
> Heaven's perfect mystery, the king of love has sent for me
> And now you're singing over me, the Father's song.[2]

I will say more in a later chapter about the important part that songs, singing and worship play in the building up of our hearts and hope, but meanwhile I want to stay with the subject of the Fatherhood of God and how important it is that we really know as Christians that this is how he views us now. He doesn't just tolerate us, he likes us! More, he loves us! More, picking up on the lyrics of Matt Redman's song, he sings over us! And just in case you are thinking that Matt Redman has gone a bit too far with those words, possibly even being irreverent, he is quoting from the Bible, from Zephaniah 3:17:

The LORD your God is with you,
the Mighty Warrior who saves.
He will take great delight in you;
in his love he will no longer rebuke you,
but will rejoice over you with singing.

Knowing this changes everything. Suddenly prayer becomes much more than reeling off a number of requests, becoming instead an opportunity to come into the presence of our heavenly Father, and our approach to the whole Christian life becomes rooted in relationship rather than rules. That is what the Reformer Martin Luther discovered after many painful years trying to earn God's approval before discovering the wonderful truth that we are 'accepted in the beloved',[3] in Jesus and his death on our behalf. In the quote at the start of this chapter, Luther picks up on that little word *abba*, Aramaic for 'Father', from the first babblings of a little child and goes on to say how important this little word is for the Christian, especially when faced with difficulties. It was J.I. Packer who said that '"Father" is the Christian name for God'.[4] God's heart is to have a big family and is gathering sons and daughters from across the nations, and his intention is that his children grow up secure, assured of his love, care and provision.

Writing to the believers in Ephesus, Paul states the difference that becoming a Christian makes very starkly: 'You were separate from Christ, excluded from citizenship in Israel and foreigners to the covenants of the promise, without hope and without God in the world.'⁵ In other words, before we came to know Jesus as our Saviour, that was the state of our lives. We were cut off from God, excluded from his presence and from his promises, and as such, without a real and lasting hope. We were in a hopeless condition. But Paul then goes on to say in verse 13: 'But now in Christ Jesus you who once were far away have been brought near by the blood of Christ.' As a result of what Jesus accomplished on the cross, those who put their trust in him have been brought near, right into God's family, with wonderful promises over their lives and future! The apostle John invites us to contemplate this wonderful truth: 'See what great love the Father has lavished on us, that we should be called children of God! And that is what we are!'⁶

The New Testament uses a number of words to describe the transformation that takes place when we become a Christian. We are born again, forgiven, justified, atoned for, purchased, and more. But among these astonishing, rich, lofty words, there is one word for me that draws together all those other words and brings us to the very peak of the Bible's revelation of what it means to be a Christian. It is the word 'adoption'. Why? Because adoption speaks of a father's initiative in choosing someone with no rights or expectations and not only showing undeserved kindness and love, but taking the necessary steps to bring them into the intimacy of his family, bestowing a new name, rights and privileges, open access to their father and a guaranteed future inheritance in line with their father's wealth. We were not born into his family by birth. We were far away, separate from Christ, excluded foreigners, without God or hope, but when we put our trust in Jesus we were brought right into God's inner circle; we became family. Adopted!

I have some dear friends who have spent much of their lives working with orphans in China. Because of the one-child policy introduced in China in the 1980s to limit population growth, many babies born deformed, or a girl when a boy was wanted, were abandoned. I have visited their orphanage on the outskirts of Beijing several times and witnessed the beautiful sight of these little children being cared for, prayed for and given medical help while waiting to be adopted. My friend Byron described to me what happens when a child is chosen for adoption. Once formalities and legalities are finalized, the adopting parents, who could be anywhere in the world, send pictures of themselves and their home, along with photos of the place where they live and so on, so that the little child will have some idea of what lies ahead. And so the day comes when the news is announced that a particular child is to be adopted and the photos of their future parents and their home are presented. In Byron's words, 'They become the little superstar of the moment! This is the day that they have longed for: they have seen it happen to other little children in the orphanage and have longed for it to be their turn. Now it is their day and they can proudly say, "I've got a family!"'

What a beautiful picture of what it means to become a Christian! In a moment they have gone from being one of many who have been abandoned, seemingly unwanted and facing a very uncertain future, to having been chosen, an object of love, with parents coming to find them and take them home, giving them a new family name and providing for their needs. These truths are life-changing! There is much security to be found in the knowledge that God in his love and mercy sought me when I had no thought or appetite for him, that for some inexplicable reason he desired to lay hold of me and bring me into his family, sending his Son to die on my behalf to bring it about. And if that wasn't enough, he has sent his Spirit, the Spirit of adoption, to bear witness, to give us assurance, living proof of our acceptance, our sonship, welling up within us in such a way that we cry out (in a rather undignified way, it has to be said!): '*Abba*! Daddy! Father!' It is worth quoting this important verse in full:

> For you did not receive the spirit of slavery to fall back into fear, but you have received the Spirit of adoption as sons, by whom we cry, 'Abba! Father!' The Spirit himself bears witness with our spirit that we are children of God . . .
>
>   *Rom. 8:15–16*, ESV

Commenting on this verse, scholar Douglas Moo says, 'Paul's description of the Spirit's work in conferring sonship forms one of the most beautiful pictures of the believer's joy and security anywhere in Scripture.' He continues:

> . . . we have not only the status, but the heart of sons . . . In using the verb 'crying out,' Paul stresses that our awareness of God as Father comes not from rational consideration nor from external testimony alone but from a truth deeply felt and intensely experienced . . . In adopting us, God has taken no half measures; we have been made full members of the family and partakers of all the privileges belonging to members of that family.[7]

Well-known Bible teacher and writer Martyn Lloyd-Jones devotes seven chapters of his commentary on Romans 8 to this one verse! They are well worth reading. He too speaks highly of the implications of this truth in the life of the Christian:

> The receiving of the Spirit of adoption is a very special form or type of assurance . . . It is the assurance that a Christian has who is aware within himself of the Spirit of adoption that makes him

cry 'Abba, Father' . . . This is real enjoyment of the Christian life –
having the Spirit of adoption, whereby we cry, 'Abba, Father'. Not
merely believing it, and persuading ourselves! We know it, we can
be more certain of it than anything else.[8]

Before going to the cross, Jesus promised his disciples that he
would not leave them as orphans, bereft of his reassuring and
loving presence. Instead, he promised that he would come
to them.[9] I do not think that he was referring to his resurrection and subsequent appearances, as they only lasted for
forty days, after which he ascended, and it would have meant
that they were once more left orphaned. I believe Jesus was
speaking of the coming of the Holy Spirit, the Spirit of adoption, whose presence in their lives was to make a radical difference. In fact, Jesus assured them that the Holy Spirit, the
Comforter, would remain/abide (*meno* – there's that important word again) with them and in them.[10] Instead of a sense
of abandonment and fear about the future, they would have
an overwhelming sense of the Lord's presence with them, em-
boldening them for the challenges ahead, even to the point of
facing death for their Lord.

I have deliberately spent time in this chapter focusing on
this wonderful truth of our adoption into God's family and on
the Holy Spirit, the Spirit of adoption, because being assured
of this on a daily basis is literally life-changing – to wake each
morning with the realization and assurance that your heavenly
Father welcomes you into his presence and loves to hear your
voice, warms your devotion, fuels your prayers and prompts
your worship. And all because for some unfathomable reason
he chose you, wanting you to be his, and gave his Son to bring
it about. What provision God has made for his children! It
is often only when we come to a point in our lives when we

realize how much we need our heavenly Father's presence and help that we discover him to be all that we need – especially when things don't work out the way we would like them to.

I was praying for the cancer to go, that I would be healed, but that was not what happened. Amazingly, the cancer has not spread any further, even though I do have a secondary tumour. Instead, here I am, more than twelve years later, in pretty good shape! More to the point, these last twelve years or so have been a journey of discovery for me as I have gained a richer perspective, not only in regards to the things in life that matter and things that really don't matter at all, but also as I have learned to value each day as a gift from my heavenly Father and to rely less on my own strength and more on his. I have had some very special moments along the way, to the point that I have found myself saying on occasions that I am glad that I have had this thorn of cancer in my body because, like Paul with his thorn in the flesh, I too have discovered that the words of the Lord are true: 'My grace is sufficient for you, for my power is made perfect in weakness.'[11] In saying that, I am in no way saying that cancer is a good thing. It isn't. It is horrible, ugly and destructive. But our heavenly Father can and does use these painful moments in our lives to draw us closer to himself and awaken us to the things that matter most.

5

Finding Hope in Hard Places

What if my greatest disappointments
Or the aching of this life
Is the revealing of a greater thirst this world can't satisfy
What if trials of this life
The rain, the storms, the hardest nights
Are your mercies in disguise

Laura Story, 'Blessings'[1]

I have been privileged to see and hear about a number of wonderful instances of God graciously healing people, and so I was expectant of healing for myself. As a church leader believing in the wonderful gifts of the Spirit that Jesus has given to his church, I have a number of friends whom God has used wonderfully to bring healing to sick individuals. And so I asked for prayer, trusting for healing. We started a small weekly prayer group made up of dear friends who would stand with Angie and myself through this ordeal. But healing didn't come and so the treatment began; seven weeks of radiotherapy, travelling to the hospital each day for yet another session. Although healing did not come, what did come were some very special, unexpected moments that have impacted me greatly; glimpses of God's grace that have made me very aware of his care for me and his presence with me, especially in my moments of need.

One such unexpected moment came when I was travelling across London on the Underground. I had just been discharged from a hospital in north London where I had undergone a particularly unpleasant operation (brachytherapy, for those who know about these things!). It was just before Christmas and so rather than travelling the hundred or so miles home to Norwich by car, we agreed that Angie would come and meet me and together we would travel home by train. The only problem was that I felt pretty unwell and could hardly walk. And the tube was crowded. Part way through the journey I happened to look at a passenger standing a few feet away and thought to myself that he looked rather like a dear friend of mine who was at that time living in Beijing. I was just musing that perhaps there was someone in the world somewhere or other who looks like me (drugs can do strange things to you!) when our eyes met and a knowing look came over his face. To our amazement, it was indeed my friend Phil who had unexpectedly had to travel home from Beijing the day before! He quickly saw that I wasn't in the best of shape and asked if he could pray for me! So there, on that crowded train, this dear friend prayed for me! In my moment of great need, my heavenly Father had sent help and encouragement just when I needed it, on a train in the middle of a vast city! What are the chances? Such is the kindness of God. A wonderful glimpse of grace.

Another unexpected moment came one night after a particularly nasty operation. Lying awake in the early hours, I was in a lot of pain. I put my earphones on and started to look for one of my worship playlists that I have on my phone. But before I could find one, Classic FM came on, and I heard the words of Scripture being sung. It was a precious moment, the

Lord whispering his promises in my ear through a motet by
Karl Jenkins based on the words from Revelation, on a secular
radio station:

> And God shall wipe away all tears from their eyes; and there shall
> be no more death, neither sorrow, nor crying, neither shall there
> be any more pain: for the former things are passed away.
>
> *Rev. 21:4, KJV*

Another glimpse of grace. The strange thing is that you discover in those moments that it is possible to know tears of pain
and tears of joy both at the same time. We really can know the
joy of the Lord alongside physical pain and difficulty, and it is
all the sweeter *because* of the difficulty of the moment because
the kindness of God is coming to us just when we need it most.
So, if we want to find hope in hard places, it is important that
we are looking in the right direction – and that is away from
ourselves, lest we fall into self-pity. Far better to be looking for
glimpses of grace which will surely come to us, because it is in
the moments of our weakness that we discover that God's grace
is at hand and is wonderfully sufficient for us.

One of the challenges we all face at painful moments, be it
physical pain or otherwise, is the very real temptation of falling into self-pity. I became aware of this danger very early on
in my journey with cancer. I remember walking around a su-
permarket doing some shopping soon after my diagnosis and
randomly looking at people and thinking, 'Why is it that they
don't have cancer and I do?' while knowing absolutely nothing
about them! It was of course, totally foolish, but worse, I realized, it fed a sense of self-pity.

If you have ever read *The Pilgrim's Progress*, John Bunyan's
portrayal of the Christian life in the form of an allegory, you

will be familiar with one of the first snares that Christian
stumbled into on his journey. It was a bog, aptly named the
Slough of Despond where, we are told, he and fellow travel-
ler Pliable 'wallowed for a time, being grievously bedaubed
with the dirt . . . Pliable began to be offended, and angrily
said to his fellow, "Is this the happiness you have told me of all
this while?"',[2] and with that gave up and went home. What a
graphic description of what can happen if we allow ourselves
to wallow in self-pity! How quickly our mood can sink and our
joy be gone. The problem is, when we go through challenging
circumstances such as illness, our friends quite understandably
will want to come and express their care and sympathy for us,
but they are not always very wise in how they do that. If, for
instance, a well-meaning friend comes to you with words such
as, 'Oh, poor you, that is terrible and so sad!', that really will
not help because you already know how rotten it is and do
not need reminding. All it will do is encourage self-pity as you
start to agree with them, thinking, 'Yes, you are right, it *is* terrible, poor me!' What we do need in those moments is friends
who will just put an arm around us and express their love and
support.

As previously mentioned, it is now more than twelve years
since I was first diagnosed with cancer and amazingly I am still
alive and well, much to the surprise of my oncologist! Along
the way I have had countless scans and in excess of twenty operations, but God has been very gracious to me and although
the cancer has persisted, he has not allowed it to spread in the
way it was expected to. More importantly, I have had many
glimpses of God's grace and kindness towards me. It would be
true to say that through my battle with cancer I have come to
see my life differently, with a greater awareness of eternity. I
now live in the moment to a greater degree, valuing each day as

a gift to be appreciated and used well rather than taking it for granted or squandering it through moodiness. You may have heard the saying that the only people who are really alive are those who have cancer. I have come to value and appreciate friendships and those I love more highly, seeking not to take them for granted. But most of all, I have come to see that this life is just the prelude; it is short, and because Jesus conquered death, those who have put their trust in him have the sure future hope that the best is yet to come. Death holds no fear for me any more. It is not what it used to be because our hope wins, and I look forward to the day when I will see Jesus face to face.

Meanwhile, I am learning to lean harder on him in my weakness, discovering that the more I have to rely on him, the more I find him to be faithful. I asked him to heal me all those years ago, but he said to me what he said to the apostle Paul: '"My grace is sufficient for you, for my power is made perfect in weakness." Therefore I will boast all the more gladly about my weaknesses, so that Christ's power may rest on me.'[3]

What? Boast about weakness? That sounds crazy and slightly masochistic. It is one thing to endure weakness, but boast about it? Is Paul exaggerating or being super-spiritual? No, I don't think so. It sounds crazy to our ears because it is the exact opposite of what our culture teaches us. The world around us encourages us to believe in ourselves, to be confident in who we are, to believe that we have within us the strengths and abilities to reach our true potential, and it is seen as a sign of weakness to rely on others. But that is not the way of the Christian. As followers of Jesus, we are called not to put our faith in ourselves, in our own abilities and resources (which will ultimately fail us) but in our Lord and Saviour, Jesus – to follow him whose path to fruitfulness and joy took him to the cross before rising in glory. What Paul is saying is that he gladly embraces situations that cause him to feel weak and possibly vulnerable because they stop him from being self-reliant; he must die to self, and is forced to draw on the power of the risen Lord Jesus Christ, who is ready and waiting to come to his aid.

J.I. Packer, who I have already quoted, died in 2020, and interestingly, as he neared the end of his life and experienced some of the challenges of the ageing process, he wrote a book entitled *Weakness is the Way*:

> Men and women of the world draw on their talents and ingenuity to map out for themselves paths of strength and success in worldly terms. Christians plan paths of faithfulness to Christ knowing that these involve both apparent and real weakness. And they settle for this on the understanding that journeyings of faithfulness, which please their Lord as of now, lead to final glories.[4]

Sometimes it can take challenges in our lives to shake us out of our complacency, remind us of the frailty and passing nature of this life, and bring our focus to bear on the magnificent future that Jesus has won for us.

The words quoted at the start of this chapter are from a song entitled 'Blessings', written by Laura Story. Shortly after their marriage, her husband, Martin, was diagnosed with a disabling brain tumour, the consequences of which turned their lives upside down. The point she makes in the song is that 'normal' appears to offer us a strong, secure foundation for our lives, but as we all discover sooner or later, 'normal' just doesn't hold up when difficulties come our way. In fact, those very difficulties can be God's way of drawing us away from the false promise of security that 'normal' offers, and into an unshakable life and future that God has for us. We just need to make sure that we are looking in the right direction, away from ourselves and our self-pity and towards the one who has loved us with an everlasting love, whose 'grace has brought us safe thus far' and whose 'grace will lead us home'.[5] I conclude this chapter with the chorus of her song:

What if your blessings come through raindrops
What if Your healing comes through tears
What if a thousand sleepless nights are what it takes to know You're near
What if trials of this life are Your mercies in disguise.[6]

6

Hope in the Face of Death

Death is the Great Interruption, tearing loved ones away from us, or us from them.
Death is the Great Schism, ripping apart the immaterial parts of our being and sundering a whole person, who was never meant to be disembodied, even for a moment.
Death is the Great Insult, because it reminds us, as Shakespeare said, that we are worm food.

Tim Keller[1]

The culture we live in does not handle death very well, which is hardly surprising when there is little certainty in an afterlife and little thought given to it. Death is a subject to be avoided for fear of spoiling the present by making us feel morbid. A secular society that has been fed the theory of evolution, that all life evolved by chance and is no more than a random conglomeration of matter that will one day rot, if consistent cannot offer any hope whatsoever beyond death. Consequently, death is a subject to be avoided as long as possible.

The truth is that death really ought to be a matter of great importance for all of us, even if we are in good health, because the old saying is true: nothing is certain in life except death and taxes.[2] Unfortunately, unlike our predecessors, those of us currently living in more developed nations live in a culture that has the illusion that a long, comfortable life with good health is the birthright of everyone. So comfortable have we all become, including Christians, that we feel able to live our lives without really thinking about death very much at all – until it comes close or something like the COVID-19 pandemic happens. Recently, I noticed the number of deaths due to COVID-19 here in the UK passed the 100,000 mark. Worldwide the figure is nearing 2.5 million. Death is very much in the news. The *Sunday Times* ran an article with the title: 'It's far too late to think about death when you're dying – Let's do it now'.[3] It would seem that this is a moment when God is getting our attention.

Two incidents happened that caused me to draw more deeply on the subject of the Christian's future hope. The first was when I was diagnosed with cancer. The second was when our daughter, Ali, suddenly became ill, almost three years ago now, while away on holiday with her husband, Dan, and children, Annabelle and Luke. They were camping in Devon and Ali woke one morning feeling uncomfortable, and felt it was sufficient to seek out a doctor. A visit to the local surgery quickly led to being admitted to hospital the same day, the doctor suspecting that her discomfort might be due to something more serious than gallstones. We got a call from Ali and Dan that evening from her hospital bed, explaining the situation, saying that she would be having some scans and that they would know the results the following day. I am finding it hard to type these words three years later.

We of course set about praying fervently that the results would show that nothing serious was wrong. The call came the next day. The results of the scans showed that our precious daughter had secondary cancer of the liver and primary breast cancer. We were devastated. It had all happened so suddenly – one minute she was well, the next very seriously ill. They drove home with their two little children that evening and we immediately called our friends to pray. We knew how to do this; after all, I had faced cancer and by God's grace, through prayer and the help of medics, I had come through. So we gave ourselves to prayer, fervent prayer, the only way parents know how to pray for their children when they are seriously ill. We cried out to God for our daughter, asking him to heal her, reminding him that her young children needed her, and that her husband, a church leader, needed her.

Hospital appointments began almost immediately, and every time we drove the twenty-mile journey to visit, Angie and I prayed all the way there and back. We didn't let up. But Ali got worse. That period of our lives remains a painful time for us to recall. Just two weeks later, on the Monday, we drove over to visit her again, now in hospital. When we arrived, she was clearly feeling uncomfortable, attached to various drips, and conversation was getting difficult. In the evening as we left, we kissed Ali goodbye, saying that we would be back in the morning. It was to be the last time we saw her alive.

Just a few hours later, back at home, the phone rang. It was our son, Steve, calling from the hospital. He had felt prompted to drive over after work to see his sister and join Dan at her bedside. 'Dad, mum, come quickly, Ali is struggling to breathe!' We drove to the hospital faster than we ought, arriving to meet Steve at the entrance, in tears. 'I'm sorry, you're too late; she's gone!' We stood there, at the entrance to the hospital, hugging each other and weeping uncontrollably, oblivious to the comings and goings around us.

A while later, having composed ourselves, we went into Ali's room and, gathering around her bed with her husband,

Dan, and his parents, we somehow found ourselves singing these words:

> When I stand in glory
> I will see His face,
> And there I'll serve my King forever,
> In that holy place.

> Thank you, O my Father
> For giving us your Son,
> And leaving your Spirit 'til
> Your work on earth is done.[4]

Somehow we found our way home in a state of shock, weeping in our great sorrow. Had this really happened? Would we really never again see our precious daughter, Ali, in this life? I don't remember sleeping much that night, but I do remember waking early the next morning to the awful truth of what had happened, and realizing that our lives would never be the same again.

Death is ugly. It robs, it separates, it stings. Jesus hated death and wept at his friend Lazarus's tomb, even though he presumably knew that he was going to raise him from the dead. So why did he weep? Maybe it was seeing the grieving of Martha and Mary and others gathered at the loss of a brother and friend.[5] Or maybe he wept because he was feeling the pain and sorrow of all the deaths that evil inflicts in this fallen world. I am glad that Jesus wept, because it helps us as we weep our loss to realize that he knows how it feels.

Of course, as Christians we do have the wonderful, priceless assurance that death has been defeated, that on the cross, Jesus overcame death, taking our sin, the sting of death upon

himself. He rose from death on the third day, defeating it forever for all who put their trust in him, fulfilling what he spoke
of to Nicodemus, in what has become one of the best-known
verses in the Bible, John 3:16: 'For God so loved the world
that he gave his one and only Son, that whoever believes in
him shall not perish but have eternal life.' In the familiar words
heard at most Christian funerals, the apostle Paul reassures us
that there is a day coming, resurrection day, at the last trumpet:

> . . . For the trumpet will sound, the dead will be raised imperish-
> able, and we will be changed. For the perishable must clothe itself
> with the imperishable, and the mortal with immortality. When
> the perishable has been clothed with the imperishable, and the
> mortal with immortality, then the saying that is written will come
> true: 'Death has been swallowed up in victory.' 'Where, O death,
> is your victory? Where, O death, is your sting?'
>
> *1 Cor. 15:52–55*

But that is speaking of a day in the future, 'at the last trumpet'
(v. 52); 'when he comes . . . the end will come' (vv. 23–24).
This is 'The day of the Lord' as it is called elsewhere in the
Bible,[6] or the last day, when Jesus will return in great glory to
raise all the dead on judgement day, to bring about justice and
right wrongs in a new, renewed heaven and earth.[7]

It was only quite recently that I realized that those verses do
not say that for the Christian death has already lost its sting,
but rather that the day is coming, a glorious day when trumpets announce the return of Jesus, when all will be made new
and the dead will be raised. Then, and not until then, will the
saying quoted from Hosea 13:14 come true, *Death is swallowed
up in victory: death, your sting has gone.* Until then, death continues to sting, even though we, as it were, know the end of

the story. So let me assure you, it is not wrong or unspiritual to weep, to feel the loss of dear ones. As I mentioned, Jesus wept at the tomb of his friend Lazarus, even though he knew that he would be raised to life again.

In his book *A Grief Observed*, C.S. Lewis likens bereavement to an amputation. In answer to the question 'Are you getting over it?' he wrote:

> To say the patient is getting over it after an operation for appendicitis is one thing; after he's had his leg off it is quite another. After that operation either the wounded stump heals or the man dies. If it heals, the fierce, continuous pain will stop. Presently he'll get back his strength and be able to stump about on his wooden leg. He has 'got over it.' But he will probably have recurrent pains in the stump all his life, and perhaps pretty bad ones; and he will always be a one-legged man. There will be hardly any moment when he forgets it. Bathing, dressing, sitting down and getting up again, even lying in bed, will all be different. His whole way of life will be changed. All sorts of pleasures and activities that he once took for granted will have to be simply written off. Duties too. At present I am learning to get about on crutches. Perhaps I shall presently be given a wooden leg. But I shall never be a biped again.[8]

So with us; we weep because the gift of a dear one has been taken from us. As I mentioned earlier, it is now around three years since our daughter, Ali, died and we continue to have moments when memories of her bring sadness to our hearts and tears to our eyes, even though we know the end of the story, because that is then and this is now and right now we feel the sadness of being so suddenly separated from our daughter. Parents are not supposed to bury their children; it ought to be the other way round.

In our culture with its comparative stability, comforts and excellent medical care we are shielded to a great extent from death in a way that previous generations could only have imagined. For them death was much closer to home, be it due to a much higher infant mortality, shorter life expectancy because of poverty, lack of healthcare or just the more precarious nature of life. The same would be true for people in many parts of the world today who live in less fortunate or more turbulent circumstances. We in the West, however, are able to push death to the recesses of our minds in the fairly safe assumption that we will have our 'threescore years and ten'[9] before we have to think about it. And if we do bring up the subject of death, we are told that we are being morbid. In fact, if we are wise, we will all give this important subject some serious thought because our future destiny depends on it. To think about death before we are faced with it is not foolish or morbid, it is essential. Martyn Lloyd-Jones puts it bluntly: 'To me there is nothing more fatuous about mankind than the statement that to think about death is morbid. The man who refuses to face facts is a fool.'[10] When we are caught up in the busyness and attractions of life, death and things of eternity can seem far away, but if someone close to you suddenly dies, the gap between this life and eternity suddenly becomes much narrower.

So, what lies ahead for us at death? We have already said that for the Christian there is the expectation that there is a day coming, the 'day of the Lord' as it is often called in the Bible, when Jesus will return in great glory, intervening in world history to usher in a new heaven and new earth. On that day, the Bible tells us, the dead will be raised, wrongs will be righted, tears wiped away and everything made new. There will of course be a very solemn aspect to that day about which Jesus frequently warned us. The righting of wrongs involves judgement as well as recompense, and Jesus very clearly warned us that on that day all our deeds will be brought to light – the good, the bad, the ugly – and that we will be judged for our sins.[11] What a relief, what a joy for the Christian who has been to the cross and put their trust in what Jesus achieved for us there, paying the price so that they can say with Martin Luther '"My sin is not mine." . . . "My sins have been transferred to Christ; He has them." . . . Note the wonderful exchange: One man sins, another pays the penalty; one deserves peace, the other has it. The one who should have peace has chastisement, while the one who should have chastisement has peace.'[12] What wonderful words! What good news! What a great hope for the future! But what happens to us if we die before that day? Will we be conscious or will we slip into some sort of coma, nothingness, while we wait?

Soul sleep is the belief that at the point of death our souls slip into a 'sleep' while we await the 'day of the Lord' when Jesus comes, at which point we will be raised with new bodies. The inscriptions on many tombstones would seem to imply this: 'Rest in peace', and so on. Is that to be our hope, our expectation at death, to slip into some sort of unconsciousness? I don't think so; neither do I believe that to be what the Bible teaches, and I am glad about that because it sounds like nothingness to me. The reason some have adopted this idea is because the New Testament does use the phrase 'fell asleep' to refer to people dying. For instance, when describing the death of Stephen, the first Christian martyr, we read in Acts 7:59–60: 'While they were stoning him, Stephen prayed, "Lord Jesus, receive my spirit." Then he fell on his knees and cried out, "Lord, do not hold this sin against them." When he had said this, he fell asleep.' Paul uses the same language when speaking of death when writing to believers in Corinth and Thessalonica.[13] So why use that language? I believe it is because Paul and Luke, who wrote those words, were very aware that death is no longer what it used to be because of what Jesus has achieved for us by his death and resurrection, and they are making that point. Death is not the end. But I do not believe the Bible teaches soul sleep for the following reasons.

Paul confidently tells us that he viewed death as gain: 'For to me, to live is Christ and to die is gain' (Phil. 1:21) and that he would 'prefer to be away from the body and at home with the Lord' (2 Cor. 5:8). If death were nothingness, unconsciousness, it would not be gain; in fact, it would be a lot less than what we have at present. Also, thinking of the account of the stoning of Stephen, if you read the verses just before he 'fell asleep', Luke records that Stephen cried out, 'I see heaven open' (v. 56)! Lastly and most convincingly you may recall that when Jesus was hanging on the cross, one of the criminals asked Jesus to remember him when entering his kingdom, to which Jesus replied: 'Truly I tell you, today you will be with me in paradise.'[14] This fits perfectly with Jesus' encouragement to his disciples before going to the cross, not to be troubled by what was to happen to him because he was going to 'prepare a place' for them in his Father's house where there are many mansions, rooms, where they would be reunited with him.[15] This magnificent truth has enabled countless Christians down the generations to face the moment of death with the sure, imminent hope of being with the Lord! What an encouragement in the face of death! What reassurance in the face of loss! It certainly gives Angie and me great joy in our grief to know that our dear daughter is not in a state of unconsciousness, nothingness, awaiting a day yet to come, but rather, she is in heaven, in the presence of her Saviour, the Lord Jesus Christ whom she loved and lived for through her life. And that same hope inspires me and warms my heart when I think of dying, in the same way that I believe it did the hearts of the first Jesus followers we read about in the Bible and many generations since.

But I am getting ahead of myself. Although we comforted ourselves with the thought that our daughter was no longer in any pain and that she was with her Lord and Saviour Jesus, nevertheless we were feeling considerable pain in our great loss, and before long the questions began:

Why didn't you heal her, Lord?

Why didn't I die? I'm in my sixties now and ready now to die and be with you.

Why wasn't this cancer discovered sooner?

What about her husband and children?

And we wept.

7

Why, O Lord?

To cry is human, but to lament is Christian.

Mark Vroegop[1]

Surely it is wrong to question God, isn't it? Does it not show a
lack of trust, of faith in God? Isn't the mature Christian way not
to allow oneself to ask such questions but to silence them and
rise above them? While it is definitely the case that in many circumstances it can be unhelpful to entertain unbelieving doubts
and questions, and it is indeed important as Christians that we
ground our thinking in wonderful truths, nevertheless when it
comes to grief and our grieving the loss of loved ones, I have
come to see that it is actually helpful to express our questions.
And it is biblical! In fact, there is a word for it: lament.

There are various theories on the subject of grief and grieving, what to expect, how many stages there are, what order
they come in, how long they last, and so on. Some say there
are five stages – denial, anger, bargaining, depression, acceptance – others suggest that there are seven stages, and then there
is difference of opinion as to the order that they occur. These
theories suggest that grief, like an illness, is something that one
just needs to accept and succumb to, go with the flow, endure
passively until it passes and you come out the other end.

While I certainly agree that there are different emotions that we experience when we grieve the loss of a loved one, I do not think that it is helpful just to succumb to them passively in the expectation that they will pass. Contrary to the popular saying, time is not necessarily a great healer. The passing of time might just as easily leave you depressed, withdrawn, bitter or broken. It is not unusual for marriages to collapse in the wake of the loss of a child, due to the sheer weight of the emotional trauma on the relationship. The Bible shows us a better way to walk the path of grief, a way that will keep us safe through our turbulent thinking and questions, and bring us through, stronger in our faith. It teaches us to lament.

I have already mentioned the 'what if' questions that started to present themselves to us when I was diagnosed with cancer; after Ali's death it was not long before we inevitably asked the 'Why?' question: 'Why was she not healed?' 'Why is this happening to *us*?' 'Why, Lord, have you let this happen to this precious family?' Why? Why? Why? Was that lack of faith, trust on our part? No, it was our faith grappling with the awful thing that had happened. The important thing is what we do with those questions. We can perhaps try to rationalize what has happened and search for a reason that will satisfy our questions. Well-meaning Christian friends might even offer their suggestions along these lines in an attempt to encourage us. We quickly realized that this route was not a profitable one because no matter how hard we tried, no thought-up answer was sufficient to offset the sadness that we felt at the thought of our loss, Dan's loss and that of those little children, Annabelle and Luke, left without their mum.

As an aside, I would advise that if you are unsure how best to comfort and encourage a friend who has suffered loss, take note from Job's 'comforters'.[2] The best thing they did in the whole of that painful narrative was just to sit with their friend for a whole week without saying a word. Don't be afraid to just 'weep with those who weep', as it tells us in Romans 12:15 (ESV). So, returning to the question of what to do with those questions. If trying to rationalize compelling answers doesn't suffice, what can we do with them? The Bible's answer is to take them to our heavenly Father, and that is what it means to lament.

Lament literally means 'I wail, weep' (from the Latin, *lamentor*), and has come to mean giving passionate expression to sorrow or grief. I won't dwell on the fact that whereas those of a Latin background might be more familiar with the expressing of emotion, us Brits have often inherited the idea that it is more appropriate to button it and bury it with a stiff upper lip. Such an approach to grieving is not very helpful, nor is it biblical. So let me get to the point.

The book of Psalms, strategically placed slap-bang in the middle of the Bible such that it is where the Bible will most naturally open, has much to teach us when it comes to talking with God. Whereas most of the other books in the Bible have to do with God speaking to us, in the psalms David (along with others at times) shows us how to talk to God, through every circumstance of life and not just when we feel blessed.

I began Chapter One with the opening verse of Psalm 130 in the graphic words of *The Message* translation: 'Help, GOD – the bottom has fallen out of my life!' There are many other psalms where David appears to unashamedly question God. Look at his blunt words in Psalm 13:1–4:

> How long, LORD? Will you forget me for ever?
> How long will you hide your face from me?
> How long must I wrestle with my thoughts

and day after day have sorrow in my heart?
How long will my enemy triumph over me?

Look on me and answer, LORD my God.
Give light to my eyes, or I will sleep in death,
and my enemy will say, 'I have overcome him,'
and my foes will rejoice when I fall.

He is clearly feeling abandoned, possibly physically wounded, and overwhelmed by sorrow. It could have been when he was on the run from King Saul or possibly from his own son, Absalom. It was a desperate moment. But the point is, he is crying out to God, and there is no better place to take our questions and desperate thoughts! See what happens next, in the following verses:

But I have trusted in Your lovingkindness;
My heart shall rejoice in Your salvation.
I will sing to the LORD,
Because He has dealt bountifully with me.

I deliberately chose to use the NASB 1995 translation here because it always translates the Hebrew word *hesed*, which is the word for God's covenant love, with the word 'lovingkindness', which I think is a wonderfully descriptive way to depict God's love for us. My spell checker tries to tell me that there is no such word and I enjoy telling it otherwise!

In his desperation David is talking to God, and as he does so, prompted by the Holy Spirit, I suggest, he is reminded of the wonderful, dependable, unfailing covenant-keeping love of God. This is what biblical lament does for us as we take our sorrows, hurts and questions to the Lord. The book of Psalms is so helpful in teaching us to express our hearts fully to the Lord, whatever the circumstances, and that is why I use them almost on a daily basis. Certainly, through the difficult days that we have navigated they have been a great comfort. Even now, almost three years later, I still at times have those tearful conversations with the Lord, sort of questioning, 'Why, Lord?' but basically expressing my sorrow. It is often in the context of thoughts about our grandchildren Annabelle and Luke, who we make a priority of seeing often but who are also a constant reminder to us of Ali – especially Annabelle, who looks so very much like her. I think that those conversations, those laments are good and helpful because they are not hopeless musings more likely to leave one depressed than encouraged; they are honest, open conversations with a heavenly Father who I know cares deeply for us, and whose lovingkindness towards us I am certain of, and like the psalmist, I usually end up worshipping.

Through this period of what could be called our lament, God has been good to us. As well as the strengthening of our future hope, we have been blessed by hope closer to home – the birth of a beautiful baby girl, Thea Alison Hope, to our son's wife Natalie, just four months after Ali's death. So special, and a great cause for celebration! Throughout this period Steve and Natalie, who live here in Norwich, have been a huge joy and support to Angie and myself, as we have walked the path of our loss together, us our daughter and Steve his little sister. We have had precious family times together, sharing memories with fondness, laughter and tears. I remember in the early days wondering how long grieving lasts, wishing that the sense of pain and loss would just go and that we could get through this time and get back to normal. As time has gone on, I have begun to realize that actually we don't want to 'get over' Ali's death and get back to busy normal. Yes, we certainly want to move on from feeling distraught, but we don't want to forget her; we want, every so often, to talk about her, to remember her and share memories and special moments, and with Steve and Natalie we have been able to do that together.

Another unexpected blessing in those early days was a surprising one – the COVID-19 lockdown! While this was a very trying period for most, restricting lives in so many ways, for us it has some very good memories. On the day before lockdown, Steve had been listening to all the technicalities of what one could and couldn't do and he called us to say that it would be legal (and certainly very helpful) for Dan, Annabelle and Luke to come and live in our home. A quick phone call with Dan's parents, Stuart and Lynn, who happen to live next door (it's a long story!) and it was all arranged. Dan and the children would spend half the week living with us in our home, and then go next door to spend the second half of the week with Stuart and Lynn. Perfect. And what a joy those months were! Yes, the house was pretty chaotic, what with home schooling, early starts to the day and never a dull moment, but it was wonderful, having extended quality time with the children and with Dan, who has become very dear to us. We will forever have some special memories of those days that God gave us, like the afternoon a young deer somehow found its way into the garden and couldn't find the way out. Dan nobly tried to corral the poor creature towards the garden gate, much to the great amusement of us all! In the end he gave up and it spent the night in our garden.

Looking back, God was good to us through those early months after our great loss, blessing us in unexpected ways through our family and church friends. Sometimes it was in quite unlikely ways, such as lockdown, or through unlikely people committing to pray for us daily, or unexpected deliveries of cake on the doorstep. But through it all, we can see the fingerprints of our heavenly Father assuring us of his constant care, and in the process, our hope for the future, our hope of heaven and what that entails has become more important to us.

Of course, we still have unanswered questions, but that is the nature of the Christian faith: trusting the one who loves us has redeemed us and will one day make all things new, and bring us into the full enjoyment of his presence. It is not as though we expected full explanations because we know that this side of eternity there will be none; rather, our questions were the overflow of our grief and our longing for God's good future, and so we would walk the beach or the countryside near our home pouring out our 'questions' and our longings, often with tears, to the Lord.

I can do no better at this point than to quote Christopher Ash, writing in the context of Job's questioning of God:

> We ought to expect that the normal Christian life will be full of unresolved waiting and yearning for God. This is the mark of a believer, of real and personal religion. So we should never be fatalists . . . We ought to say, 'What is God doing, the God who is my maker and my friend? Where is this personal God in all this? If only I could speak to him; if only I might find him.' Such directed, prayer-filled, intentional waiting is the integrating arrow of hope that holds together the authentic Christian life.[3]

In the following chapter we return to the subject of our future hope, and in particular our hope of heaven.

8

Rediscovering Heaven

Full memory flooded back, and Sam cried aloud: 'It wasn't a dream!
Then where are we?'
And a voice spoke softly behind him: 'In the land of Ithilien, and
in the keeping of the King; and he awaits you.' With that Gandalf
stood before him, robed in white, his beard now gleaming like pure
snow in the twinkling of the leafy sunlight. 'Well, Samwise, how do
you feel?' He said.
But Sam lay back, and stared with open mouth, and for a mo-
ment, between bewilderment and great joy, he could not answer.
At last he gasped: 'Gandalf! I thought you were dead! But then I
thought I was dead myself. Is everything sad going to come untrue?'
J.R.R. Tolkien, *The Lord of the Rings*[1]

If you are a *Lord of the Rings* fan, you will recognize those
words. At the climax of the story, the hero, Frodo, and his
faithful friend Sam have just faced the life-threatening horrors
of Mordor in order to destroy the fated ring. In fact, so severe has been their encounter, Sam thinks they have died. I
will say no more – read the book! The way Tolkien writes of
their experience in those moments between life and death are
beautiful. Where are they? 'In the land of Ithilien, and in the
keeping of the King; and he awaits you.' And then Sam poses

that priceless question: 'Is everything sad going to come un-true?' That sounds much like heaven to me! 'In the keeping of the King; and he awaits you'! What wonderful words and what a wonderful description of death for the Christian. My heart leaps as I contemplate those words, reminding myself that one day, at the point of death, I will have nothing to fear and much to anticipate! And everything sad becoming untrue, or perhaps I should say, glorified.

So, what does happen to Christians when they die? Various imagery has been used over the centuries, likening death to 'crossing over Jordan' as in the African-American spiritual 'Swing Low, Sweet Chariot'. This refers to the journey the Israelites made when they entered the Promised Land after first crossing the river Jordan. The other often referred-to imagery is that of arriving at the pearly gates to be met by St Peter. So what does happen to us at death while we wait for Jesus to return and raise the dead, on that great day when he wipes away all tears and makes all things new? Let me answer this impor-tant question right away, and then I will explain why I have felt passionate about writing this book.

Like the thief being crucified alongside Jesus in Luke 23, we who have put our trust in him have the sure knowledge that on that very same day we will be with Jesus in paradise, in heaven. That being the case – and I hope that I have shown that it is, indeed, what the Bible teaches – then you will understand why our expectation of heaven matters, a lot! By the way, the word 'paradise' comes from a Persian word meaning a garden, an en-closed garden, and appears elsewhere in the Bible with links to a future Garden of Eden.[2] It also appears in 2 Corinthians 12:4 and Revelation 2:7 where it refers to the heavenly realm where God is. What a comfort! What an encouragement it was for us and continues to be in our loss.

What comes to mind when you think of heaven? Clouds? Angels plucking harps? A place of stunning beauty? Several years ago, I received an invitation to go and teach at a church in Hawaii. Now, I can't say I knew exactly where Hawaii was; in fact, I had to look at a map and was surprised how far away it was – from everywhere! But I had heard that it was beautiful, the stuff of dreams, and so was immediately interested. It was winter in England, one of those cold, grey January days when the clouds come down almost to the ground and the sun has no chance of getting through. At first, I thought it might be the work of a mischievous friend, a New Year hoax to brighten a dull day, but on investigation it proved to be perfectly authentic, and so we prayed, pondered and promptly accepted the invitation.

If you have ever looked for Hawaii on a map you will know that it is a very long way away from the UK. In fact, it is some 3,000 miles from the west coast of mainland USA, so for us it required a two-hour train journey followed by a fourteen-hour flight followed by another five-hour flight, with much waiting in-between. I realize that as you read this you have absolutely no sympathy for us! And why should you? Because we have all heard rumours about how idyllic Hawaii is, with its palm trees, its clear blue sea, spectacular waves and pleasant climate. Our expectation of what lay ahead made any trial or inconvenience on the journey of little consequence at all. And we were not disappointed.

On landing in Kona, Hawaii about twenty-four hours later, weary and stiff, the flight captain woke us with the words: 'Welcome to paradise!' and as soon as the doors were opened the sweet fragrance of the Hawaiian evening air confirmed that we were indeed somewhere rather special. Challenging journey? What journey? On venturing out of the plane, instead

of being confronted with grey, utilitarian terminal buildings
I noticed a number of modest, white buildings with thatched
roofs. And instead of having to patiently wait in line we were
greeted by our delightful hosts who threw colourful, fragrant
Hawaiian *leis* around our necks! 'Welcome to paradise!' they
said. The rumours were true.

Most people find it difficult to even form a helpful and
inspiring mental image of heaven, partly as a result of those
aforementioned stereotypical images of heaven involving angels sitting on clouds plucking harps, and St Peter standing
by the pearly gates. I remember as a child on first hearing of
heaven, about streets of gold and the fact that it would go on
forever, feeling quite fearful of this harsh place where a church
service went on eternally! I knew that I was supposed to like
the idea of going there one day but I really did not. But what
if you had in your mind's eye thoughts of a place so astonish-
ingly beautiful and inviting that it couldn't fail to thrill you,
something like Hawaii or the most perfect scene that you can
imagine, but spectacularly better? What if you knew it involved
the most perfect face-to-face reunion with someone who loves
you more than you can imagine? What if you had been told
enough about that place and your part in it that the thought of
it warmed your heart with joy, even in the face of suffering? For
myself and my wife, having such an expectation for our daughter at the moment of her death and in the ongoing moments
when we miss her, it was and continues to be priceless.

I mentioned earlier *The Pilgrim's Progress*. Written by John
Bunyan in the seventeenth century while in prison, it is one of
the most widely read pieces of Christian literature ever written.
Translated into more than two hundred languages, it tells the
story of a man named Christian and his journey through life in
the form of a dream. Using allegory, John Bunyan tells of the

challenges and obstacles that Christian and his companions encounter on their journey. Having read in a book, the Bible, that
the city he lives in, the City of Destruction, was to be burned
by fire, Christian left, setting out on a journey to the Celestial
City. There is a moment towards the end of Christian's journey
when he tells of the heart-warming effect the anticipation of
heaven, the Celestial City, had on his companion, Mr Steadfast:
'the thoughts of what I am going to, and of the conduct that
waits for me on the other side, doth lie as a glowing coal at my
heart.' In Bunyan's allegory it is characters such as Pliable and
Mr Worldly-Wiseman who seek to persuade Christian to give
up the notion and discomfort of the journey and instead, to settle in the village named Morality, along with Mr Civility: 'provision is there also cheap and good; and that which will make thy
life the more happy is there to be sure, for thou shalt live by honest neighbours, in credit and good fashion.'[3] Bunyan is making
the point that there is the very real temptation for Christians to
take the comfortable option, to live for the present rather than
for the future and settle in the surrounding culture, persuading
themselves that living a good, upright life is sufficient.

In his book entitled *A Long Obedience in the Same Direction*,
Eugene Peterson alerts us to this danger, pointing out the true
nature of the Christian life:

> For recognizing and resisting the stream of the world's ways there
> are two biblical designations for people of faith that are extremely
> useful: disciple and pilgrim. Disciple says we are people who spend
> our lives apprenticed to our master, Jesus Christ . . . Pilgrim tells
> us we are a people who spend our lives going someplace . . .[4]

Unfortunately, among contemporary theologians there is now
a tendency to discourage the idea of seeing heaven as our future

destiny, a place we go to when we die. Reacting against the popular characterizing of heaven in wispy terms, with angels sitting on clouds playing harps, they prefer to think of heaven as a spiritual dimension of our lives now, a present reality rather than a future destiny. However, I believe the New Testament teaches that it is both.[5]

So keen are many theologians to get away from the idea that the Christian's hope involves going *away* from this world to a non-material place called heaven, that they run the risk of robbing us of a vital part of our future hope that previous generations of Christians have celebrated to their great encouragement. By rightly pointing out that God's ultimate plan is the making new, the re-creation of all things in a new, material heaven and earth at the return of Jesus, they tend to undermine the idea of an otherworldly heaven as a focus for our hopes and longings in the meantime. The argument goes that if we become too heavenly minded we will be of no earthly good; we will in effect become dreamers, whereas as Christians we should be focused on seeing the kingdom of heaven come on earth now. In other words, a future hope that involves a spiritual, non-material destiny away from this world will not motivate us sufficiently for the mission of the kingdom here and now. C.S. Lewis begs to differ:

> If you read history you will find that the Christians who did most for the present world were just those who thought most of the next. The Apostles themselves, who set on foot the conversion of the Roman Empire, the great men who built up the Middle Ages, the English Evangelicals who abolished the Slave Trade, all left their mark on Earth, precisely because their minds were occupied with Heaven. It is since Christians have largely ceased to think of the other world that they have become so ineffective in this.

Aim at Heaven and you will get earth 'thrown in'; aim at earth and you will get neither.[6]

Thoughts about heaven, properly understood, do not just inspire us as Christians. They also infuse heavenly joy into our hearts, strengthening us in the face of life's challenges, such as bereavement, and driving out fear in the face of sickness and death. Could it be that in our generation, by losing sight of the prize, heaven, the Eternal City, we Christians are in danger of succumbing to the voices that would encourage us to forget about the journey and settle for the ways and comforts of this life? J.I. Packer thinks so. In his little book *Laid-back Religion* he asks the question: 'Is our Christianity now out of shape? Yes, it is, and the basic reason is that we have lost the New Testament's two-world perspective that views the next life as more important than this one and understands life here essentially preparation and training for life hereafter.'[7] I think Packer is right. I saw a tweet by a friend and fellow church leader Phil Whittall recently in which he said: 'I've been saying for more than twenty years that consumerism is the biggest enemy the church has failed to fight.' How easy it is to be drawn in by the lure of advertising, to surround ourselves with comforts and provisions for our future, to settle, making our home in this world instead of realizing that it is passing away and that we were made for another.

Jesus called his first disciples with the words 'Follow me',[8] demanding a leaving behind of 'normal' and a following after. Jesus went on to warn would-be disciples not to 'store up treasures on earth'[9] but in heaven because our hearts will be drawn by what we treasure and our hearts, as pilgrims, are to be heaven-focused, not earth-focused (and also for the stark reason that this world is 'passing away'[10]). This is the 'two-world perspective' that Packer is talking about. The apostle John warns us similarly, not to 'love the world or anything in the world' because it is passing away.[11] He then goes on to explain what he means by 'the world' – 'the lust of the flesh, the lust of the eyes, and the pride of life'[12] – that is, all the things that the culture around values and trades in: our personal passions and appetites, our coveting and craving to own, our obsession with image, success and apparent security in life.

The apostle Paul alerts us to the fact that we are involved in a race, a fight that will require us to be determined and alert, keeping our eyes focused on our future hope, our prize.[13] Speaking of his own challenges, in 2 Corinthians 4 he too speaks of this 'two-world perspective', one that is seen, and one that is unseen; one that is 'momentary', and one that is eternal and glorious:

> Therefore we do not lose heart. Though outwardly we are wasting away, yet inwardly we are being renewed day by day. For our light and momentary troubles are achieving for us an eternal glory that far outweighs them all. So we fix our eyes not on what is seen, but on what is unseen, since what is seen is temporary, but what is unseen is eternal.
>
> *2 Cor. 4:16–18*

Just before he was martyred in Emperor Nero's Rome, he wrote the following words:

> Not that I have already obtained all this, or have already arrived at my goal, but I press on to take hold of that for which Christ Jesus took hold of me. Brothers and sisters, I do not consider myself yet to have taken hold of it. But one thing I do: forgetting what is

behind and straining towards what is ahead, I press on towards the goal to win the prize for which God has called me heavenwards in Christ Jesus.[14]

The writer of Hebrews catalogues a long list of men and women who did extraordinary things during their lives on earth precisely because they had caught just a glimpse of what God had promised:

> All these people were still living by faith when they died. They did not receive the things promised; they only saw them and welcomed them from a distance, admitting that they were foreigners and strangers on earth. People who say such things show that they are looking for a country of their own. If they had been thinking of the country they had left, they would have had opportunity to return. Instead, they were longing for a better country – a heavenly one. Therefore God is not ashamed to be called their God, for he has prepared a city for them.
>
> *Heb. 11:13–16*

He then continues to encourage us to follow their example and run our race with perseverance, remembering that it was the anticipation of future joy that caused Jesus to endure the cross.[15] Notice the words 'heavenwards' and 'heavenly' above in those passages of Scripture just quoted and be reminded that as Christians, we are not to be settlers but rather, visionaries whose hearts have been warmed by the longing for home, the expectation of 'a better country – a heavenly one'. We are not yet home!

9

Hope in An Uncertain World

The home of fadeless splendour
Of flowers that fear no thorn
Where we shall dwell as children,
Who here as exiles mourn.
Where we shall see God's form, his face,
Where we shall hear his voice,
Where every sound and sight will
Make the gathered saints rejoice.

Bernard of Cluny[1]

I have had the privilege of visiting some very beautiful places
in the world. I have stood beside the Niagara Falls, feeling very
small and totally overwhelmed, awed by the sight, the sound
and smell of that mighty waterfall. I can try to describe it to
you by telling you about the almost deafening roar of that huge
volume of water cascading down the 50-or-so-metre drop. Or
I could try to help you imagine the sight of that vast curtain
of water and the brilliant white foamy spray that hangs in the
air. It is stunningly beautiful. But I could also tell you about
the approximately two dozen people each year who choose this
beautiful place to attempt to commit suicide. Stunningly beautiful. But it's not home.

A few years ago, Angie discovered an idyllic location for summer holiday relaxation, on an unspoilt island in the Aegean. With its small working harbour, complete with inviting tavernas, friendly locals and gem of a beach, uncrowded and with crystal-clear water gently lapping on the shore, it was very special. Most evenings we would take a swim in the pleasantly warm waters, then sit on our loungers watching the sun slowly drop to the horizon, a blazing red ball, throwing its rays across the sea towards us as it gradually slipped away. Every evening we were treated to this wonderful performance, each one unique but equally majestic. Perfect. Little did we know that just months later that same, little-known beach was to feature on news bulletins across the world, but this time swarming with people and abandoned life rafts as thousands of migrants fled the fighting in Syria, with little children and only what they could carry, in search of somewhere in the world to call home. Stunningly beautiful. But not home.

Recently Angie and I spent a cold winter's evening watching on TV the recording of an outdoor concert. The setting was a quaint town square on a warm summer's evening with the audience filling every square inch, some sitting around tables enjoying a glass of wine, all enjoying the music in a very romantic setting. At one point the orchestra performed a particularly moving piece of music, 'Wishing You Were Somehow Here Again' from Andrew Lloyd Webber's *Phantom of the Opera*. As the soprano sang, the camera panned across the audience; there was hardly a dry eye to be seen. Men and women of all ages were literally moved to tears, some leaning across to kiss loved ones. Precious moments. On that summer's evening in that crowded little town square few could have imagined that in a matter of months such socializing in close proximity would be banned, punishable with heavy fines as the world battled to contain the coronavirus. Precious. But not home.

Why is it that a magnificent view or a stunning sunset or a particular piece of music has the ability to move us to tears? If we were just flesh and bones, a fortunate concoction of atoms and molecules that chance upon the planet for a brief moment before returning to dust, it would make no sense. But, of course, the Christian perspective is very different. Made by design and with purpose by a loving creator God in his image, we have another dimension, a spiritual dimension, a soul, an inner being. In Ecclesiastes 3:11 the Teacher tells us that: '*He [God] has made everything beautiful in its time. He has also set eternity in the human heart*'. And therein lies our problem – our longing. We see, hear or touch great beauty, but the capacity, the longing of the human heart goes beyond what can be experienced fleetingly in our material existence. C.S. Lewis addresses this difficulty in a way that few other writers do. In his book *Mere Christianity* he writes:

> A baby feels hunger: well, there is such a thing as food. A duckling wants to swim: well, there is such a thing as water. Men feel sexual desire: well, there is such a thing as sex. If I find in myself a desire which no experience in this world can satisfy, the most probable explanation is that I was made for another world.[2]

In *The Weight of Glory* he expresses something more about this inner unsettledness, our longing for home:

> Apparently then, our lifelong nostalgia, our longing to be reunited with something in the universe from which we now feel cut off, to be on the inside of some door which we have always seen from the outside, is no mere neurotic fancy, but the truest index of our real situation . . . At present we are on the outside of the world, the wrong side of the door. We discern the freshness and

purity of the morning, but they do not make us fresh and pure. We cannot mingle with the splendours we see. But all the leaves of the New Testament are rustling with the rumour that it will not always be so. Some day, God willing, we shall get in.[3]

Beautiful though this world is, it is not a perfect planet. It is broken. The Bible tells us that it has fallen from its original state and like us human beings, is in need of restoration. It is possible for some of us more fortunate people to make a place for ourselves in this world where we can live in relative comfort, surrounding ourselves with those we love, purchasing the trappings of modern life and gathering up enough capital in the bank to offer some security. But it is a false security, a security that can be gone in a moment should loved ones leave, illness appear, death strike, or markets drop. It is not home.

Ours is a privileged generation. I would be counted among the Baby Boomer generation who have never experienced the rigours and painful losses of wartime or the upheaval of regime change or the insecurity of life without healthcare. In the West, ours is a time of relative prosperity and comfort that assures most people a good education, the luxury of a rewarding career, the ability to own a home and medical care should it be needed. The upshot of all this privileged provision has been that ours has become a generation with high expectations. Many of us *expect* to have a home complete with all the comforts that our parents would have considered luxuries. We *expect* to have a job that pays well, money in the bank. And we even consider it our right to have a lifespan long enough to enjoy what we have earned and consider ourselves to deserve, in a comfortable retirement.

When the prevailing view is that there is no existence beyond death it is understandable to have such an expectation of this life, and it is possible to push all thoughts of death well into the future. But for Christians who are called to follow Jesus as disciples living for an inheritance, as pilgrims embarked on a journey, being surrounded by such privilege and provision can be a snare. It can become all too easy to misplace our attention and to settle, relying on the expectations and securities on display in this life and to think very little of the life to come. Until, that is, our world is shaken by fear-filled news, or a potentially terminal illness that threatens to cut our life and expectations short. Then we wake up to the realization of how unprepared for death and our future life we actually are.

The Bible gives us the backstory, the story behind the beauty and the brokenness of the world around us and human life. Having purposefully created the heavens, the earth and everything in it, declaring it to be good, the book of Genesis tells us that God created humankind, Adam and Eve 'in his own image'.[4] They were his image-bearers, with a capacity to know him, and he placed them in the Garden of Eden, this special place where they could enjoy walking and talking with him. But not content with this subordinate role, they chose instead to rebel against God, disregard his words and warnings, preferring to be masters of their own destiny. The rest is history. Ever since Adam and Eve disobeyed God, we have been denied Eden; paradise has been lost and life on earth has become toilsome, ending in death. But the story does not end there. The gospel's good news is that God has entered into the world in the person of Jesus Christ in order to bring us back to himself, to bring us home. He was the one who declared himself to be 'the way and the truth and the life';[5] the one who we have been searching for all our lives, who came to bring us back into harmony and a loving union with God our Father. And because Jesus rose from the grave, conquering death, he has become the 'firstfruits', as 1 Corinthians 15 tells us, the beginning of the restoration, the making new of everything in the whole cosmos, us included!

In the first creation, God began with the universe, the heavens and the earth, followed by plants, vegetation, fish, birds, all the creatures of the earth, and concluding with humankind, the pinnacle of his creation, made in his own image – that is, with a capacity to know and enjoy God. But in his plan of restoration, making all things new, it is the other way round. God has begun with restoring humankind: us. This is the wonderful theme of the whole Bible, the drama of Scripture: God in his kindness and mercy going after humankind, who have rebelled and turned their backs on him, calling, pursuing, purchasing back, redeeming through the cross and making us new, making us alive through the resurrection of Jesus Christ. The centre of the story of the Bible is God's pursuit of a big family! Michael Eaton puts it like this: 'His supreme design in this world is to bring together a people. He saves and redeems and rescues and cleans, and so makes his saved and purified people to be "the church".'[6]

The restoration has already begun! Jesus has been raised from the dead, the firstfruits of his new creation, and he is saving and redeeming and rescuing and restoring men and women of every tongue, tribe and nation to be his church, the people of his new creation. In Matthew 16:18 Jesus promised to build his church, and so as his church we have a wonderful future, growing, expanding across the nations, not always comfortable, but always taking the blessing of God to a broken world. I can't resist another great quote from Michael Eaton: 'The Kingdom – the royal activity of God – uses the church as its channel of influence out into the world.'[7]

God's plan of restoring all of creation, although begun, is very evidently not yet complete, as witnessed by the beauty yet brokenness, the preciousness yet painfulness of life in this world. We are living in an in-between time while we wait for what the Bible calls 'the day of the Lord'; when Jesus will return as a glorious, majestic, conquering King, wiping away all tears and 'making everything new',[8] the way it was always intended to be.

So it is that as Christians, having been made 'alive in Christ' through the resurrection of Jesus from the dead, we still have bodies that have a finite lifespan. Yes, one day we will have a heavenly, imperishable body, as we read in 1 Corinthians 15, when the trumpet sounds and Jesus returns to herald in the new heaven and new earth. Home at last. But this has not yet happened and we are not very good at coping with this 'already but not yet' existence. More than any previous generation, ours is an age of instant gratification – we want it *now*! And waiting is not something we do very well.

However, the good news is that we can indeed have a taste of that future now. Jesus promised his followers a glimpse, a taster of their future ahead of time, in this life, for their encouragement and assurance through the challenges of the wait! So in a measure, we can have it *now*! That is the 'living hope' that the apostle Peter was referring to in 1 Peter 1:3. That is the 'living hope' that I believe every Christian should and can have and which I want to throw the spotlight on in the chapters to come. This future-focused hope, transforming the present, is what characterized those first Jesus followers and subsequent Christians all through the centuries, giving them joy on the journey, especially in the face of hardship, persecution and death. But herein lies the problem. If we make ourselves so at home here in this world in the meantime, living as though this is the only home we will ever have and setting our hopes and finding our security in what the world around us offers, then instead of joy on the journey we will share the aches and anxieties that come with living in a world that is not the home we were created for. The apostle Paul urged the Christians in Ephesus, and us, to wake up to the reality of the present:

> The hour has already come for you to wake up from your slumber, because our salvation is nearer now than when we first believed. The night is nearly over; the day is almost here.
>
> *Rom. 13:11–12*

Often it can take the wake-up call of a health scare or a bereavement to awaken us from the contentment of a comfortable, materialistic lifestyle that can so easily dull our desire and expectation for a future home, keeping us rooted in the present.

The words at the beginning of this chapter are from a poem entitled 'The Land For Which We Long', a re-writing by Dan Jones of twelfth century writings by Bernard of Cluny, a contemporary of the better-known Bernard of Clairvaux. The thrust of the poem is to awaken Christians to the urgency of the hour. Like the apostle Paul quoted above, he was aware of the temptation for Christians to lose sight of their calling, their destiny, and like the five foolish virgins in Jesus' parable in Matthew 25:1–13, fall asleep while waiting for the arrival of the bridegroom. You might say, 'Well, surely, history makes it plain that Jesus' return is not quite so imminent.' You might even persuade yourself that Jesus cannot return just yet as there is more to take place before then. Beware! Hear the words of Jesus: 'Watch therefore, for you know neither the day nor the hour.'[9] Dear Christian, this world is passing away. Many passages of Scripture tell us so, none more forcibly than Peter in his second epistle, from which I will give you just a few words:

> . . . the day of the Lord will come like a thief. The heavens will disappear with a roar; the elements will be destroyed by fire, and the earth and everything done in it will be laid bare. Since everything will be destroyed in this way, what kind of people ought you to be? You ought to live holy and godly lives as you look forward to the day of God and speed its coming.
>
> *2 Pet. 3:10–12*

Sobering words. But what a contrast for the Christian who on that day will see Jesus' face! American actor Charles Dutton, who has starred in several movies and television shows, spent seven years in prison for manslaughter as a young man. Asked in an interview how he made the transformation from prison to a successful actor he replied that he did not decorate his cell so as to remind himself that he was not there permanently.[10] Ours is not a life of settling, of making ourselves feel too at home; instead it is one of longing, of looking forward!

I close this chapter with some more words from Bernard of Cluny:[11]

> The world is full of evil
> The hour is growing late
> Stay sober and be watchful
> For the judge is at the gate –
> The judge who comes in mercy
> The judge who comes with might
> To make an end of evil,
> to set the world to right.

When the just and gentle monarch
Shall call our bones to stand
Let guilty mortals tremble
Lest they fall into his hand

Arise, arise then child of God
Live ready for the day
Seek first your father's kingdom
As you follow Jesus' way
No more a child of darkness,
Put off the deeds of night.
Get dressed! The king is coming back!
The morning is in sight!

10

Face to Face

We will weep no more
No more tears, no more shame
No more struggle, no more
Walking through the valley of the shadow
No cancer, no depression
Just the brightness of Your glory
Just the wonder of Your grace
Everything as it was meant to be
All of this will change
When we see You face to face
Jesus, face to face

Matt Redman[1]

Seeing the faces of family or friends on a screen is good, especially when you have not seen them for a long time or live far apart and are unable to visit. Through the coronavirus epidemic we all did lots of screen time and it was a lifeline to many. But no matter how good the connection is, to actually see friends far surpasses the screen substitute. Face to face is best. Shortly after Angie and I were married, we were apart for several weeks, on different continents. I had travelled to South Africa on a trip and Angie was unable to join me for three weeks. That was before the days of the internet and mobile phones, so we had to be content with airmail letters and very occasional and expensive international phone calls. As you can imagine, as fairly newlyweds our reunion was long-awaited and very special, so when I finally caught a glimpse of Angie across the airport concourse, all the waiting was forgotten. Face to face is special: the best.

You and I have been made for a face-to-face relationship with God. Created in God's image, we are more like him than anything else in all of creation. Uniquely made with the capacity to appreciate great beauty, to be amazed, to wonder, we alone have the capacity and calling to have a relationship with God. Ours is the privilege to be awed, to relate, to communicate with, to know him! Immediately after God had created man and woman in his image, he spoke to them: 'God blessed them and said to them . . .'[2] As image-bearers we can hear, receive and know God's voice, and he ours. Genesis 3 hints at 'cool of the day'[3] conversations between Adam and Eve and God in the Garden of Eden; no hiding, no shame, no distance, just the enjoyment of face-to-face friendship. We were made for this. But then we read that this relationship was broken through Adam and Eve's self-willed disobedience. As a result, sin entered the world and paradise was lost. Adam and Eve experienced shame and hid themselves from God. They no longer enjoyed the face-to-face relationship with God for which they were made. Estranged from his presence they became wanderers, away from home, lost. But God set about the task of restoring that relationship, of bringing people like you and me back to that relationship that he intended for us.

Moving on in the story to Exodus 33, we read there about Moses. He was very privileged: 'The LORD would speak to Moses face to face, as one speaks to a friend.'[4] You probably know the story – God set about having a people again, he wanted to meet face to face again with the pinnacle of his creation and so he went after a man, Abraham, and through him the people of Israel. But there they were, held captive in Egypt. It is a picture of many people's lives today; they are captives, slaves to the culture around them. It is tedious and soul-destroying, toiling on the treadmill of a consumer culture, constantly going after the next best must-have thing that promises so much but delivers so little. But God did not leave them there. He raised up Moses and set them free, bringing them out of their captivity – a picture of our salvation as Christians; being delivered from captivity, through the Red Sea, and then, in the wilderness, living in the in-between land between Egypt and the Promised Land, they had to learn how to walk with God, how to enjoy his presence again, albeit at a distance. So God summoned Moses: 'Moses, I want you to come close, I want you to have just a little taste of what I am going to do right through creation. I want you to see my face.' Moses is invited up the mountain, and when he spoke to God face to face, something happened. His face shone – he was transformed because he had been face to face with the Lord. In fact, he had to cover his face because it was shining, dazzling to look at and frightening to those around him.

Moving on in the story, God then gave Moses a blessing, a prayer that the priests were to speak over all the people, expressing his heart towards them, and you will probably recognize the words:

> The LORD bless you and keep you; the LORD make his face shine on you and be gracious to you; the LORD turn his face towards you and give you peace.

> *Num. 6:24–26*

What wonderful words! I often pray that over the church family at King's Community Church, Norwich at the end of the Sunday meeting. It is what we were made for and it is what you and I are now invited into. Unfortunately, if you read on in the story you find that the people decided that they would rather chase other goals and goods in life and turned their backs on God. The imagery used is that of adultery; in other words, God saw this not just as a matter of disobedience to a set of rules, but as the disloyalty of a loved one. But God's pursuing love would not be frustrated. The prophets expressed God's continued heart towards his people. "'I hid my face from you for a moment, but with everlasting kindness I will have compassion on you," says the LORD your Redeemer.'[5]

A redeemer is someone who buys back, redeems something or someone to make it their own, and what a price our Redeemer paid for us! On his way to the cross, Matthew tells us: 'they spat in His face and beat Him with their fists; and others slapped Him'.[6] The irony of those words. The face that we were made to know, love and delight in, spat upon.

God is doing something beautiful; his passion and purpose is to wonderfully heal and restore the brokenness, the twistedness in both us and the world around us. He wants to bring us back to a face-to- face relationship with himself and Jesus went to the cross to bring that about. Instead of fractured lives and a cosmos in confusion, the day is coming when God will make all things new! This is the future to which all of Scripture points, the day when Jesus returns in dazzling glory to make a new heaven, new earth, when the dead are raised, with no more tears, wrongs righted and Jesus the focal point of it all! This is our future hope as Christians; a material, physical, eternal existence complete with banquets and breath-taking beauty! But alongside this wonderful material, physical hope, there is something equally important for us to know. A very personal hope, a hope that involves a restoration of that face-to-face relationship for which we were made.

If you ever doubt God's love for his people and for you personally, if you have the notion that God just puts up with you and is more likely to frown than smile when he sees you face to face, then read the following words in which God uses the metaphor of precious stones, each uniquely beautiful, to describe his chosen, redeemed people, you and me:

> O afflicted one, storm-tossed and not comforted, behold, I will set your stones in antimony, and lay your foundations with sapphires. I will make your pinnacles of agate, your gates of carbuncles, and all your wall of precious stones.
>
> *Isa. 54:11–12, ESV*

In our lives we all face storms, tragedies and disappointments, things that we did not want in our lives and which threaten to take away our focus, our gaze from the Lord Jesus. Maybe at this moment you are going through painful circumstances and your future looks hard. Maybe there is a storm that has worn you out and your hope is almost gone. But listen to what God says here: 'I will set your stones [precious, beautiful stones] in antimony.' What is antimony? It is an unusual, unlikely word, *puk* in Hebrew, which was a dark-coloured paint used by women cosmetically as eyeshadow – in 2 Kings 9:30 and Jeremiah 4:30 it is translated 'eyeshadow'. This really confuses the translators because it is not normal to set stones with eyeshadow – why would you do that? But think of the metaphor being used here; God is using the metaphor of a building to describe his chosen people and he is saying that each individual person is like a precious stone, each unique and valuable. Now as I understand it, women use eyeshadow, a dark colour, so as to set off the eyes and make them shine. So God is saying that his chosen people are not just a large crowd; rather, each one is special, bought at a price and therefore valuable, and it is his intention to see that each one shines!

Let me put that personally. God is saying to his people, individually, 'I am building something beautiful, worthy to be set off with eyeshadow because one day I am going to display you for my glory.' Why are gems so beautiful? Because they sparkle by reflecting light, and that is what you are designed to be. Just as every gem has been cut differently, making it unique, so too you and I have been cut by the circumstances of our lives, sometimes painfully, but in a way that will one day result in something of great beauty when we stand before the Lord Jesus, face to face, and his glory is reflected on those cuts. In fact, the more pressure we have been under, the more pain we have been through, the more beautifully we will reflect the glory of God.

If you are feeling the loss of a loved one, or if you have endured physical pain in life, or the pain of being denied a loving marriage or children, then ponder this thought. God is faithful and those losses and pains, like cuts on a precious stone, will result in more reflected glory when you stand one day in the presence of Jesus, face to face. It will not be a matter of compensation for things endured or lost, it will be glorification as his glory shines on those cuts.

When we come to the New Testament, John, the disciple of Jesus, tells us: 'The Word became flesh and made his dwelling among us. We have seen his glory, the glory of the one and only Son, who came from the Father, full of grace and truth.'[7] God has come close! We have seen his glory! So where did they see the bright radiance of God that Moses was allowed to glimpse for a moment? The answer is found in one of my favourite verses in the Bible: 'For God, who said, "Let light shine out of darkness," made his light shine in our hearts to give us the light of the knowledge of God's glory displayed in the face of Christ.'[8]

The God whose voice called all of creation into being, whose glorious presence you were made to know and enjoy intimately, face to face, has come close and revealed himself where? In the face of Jesus Christ! The glory of God, his overwhelming, dazzling presence is again on display and when you become a Christian, a 'Christ one', God causes his presence to shine into your heart, your inner being, and it is all in the face of Jesus Christ! On one occasion Jesus took three of his disciples up a mountain and was transfigured in front of them, his whole appearance becoming dazzlingly bright.[9] Jesus had just a while earlier asked the disciples, 'Who do people say I am?' Peter replied, 'You are the Messiah'[10] and, as if in response to Peter's recognition of who Jesus really is, they have this awesome moment of dazzling face-to-face encounter with Jesus, 'Immanuel . . . "God with us"'![11]

The Bible tells us that in taking on humanity, Jesus laid aside his glory, his majesty,[12] but in that moment his disciples are given a glimpse of the glory of God! The well-known Christmas carol 'Hark! The Herald Angels Sing' has the lines:

> Veiled in flesh the Godhead see,
> Hail th' incarnate Deity!
> Pleased as man with man to dwell,
> Jesus our Immanuel.[13]

In Moses' day, God's presence in the tabernacle had to be hidden from view by a curtain because it was so awesome, so holy, so overwhelming that the people dare not look on it. But when Jesus died on the cross we are told that the curtain in the temple hiding God's presence, his glory, from view, was torn, ripped from top to bottom![14] In other words, because of what Jesus achieved on the cross, taking on himself the sin of the world in order to redeem us, peace with God has been restored and the way back into the enjoyment of God's presence has been opened, forever! The future hope and expectation of every Christian is the enjoyment for eternity of God's presence, face to face – the very thing we were all created for and have longed for all our lives!

But this just gets better and better. The pages of the New Testament are alive with the news of the stunning consequences of Jesus' death and resurrection for us. We do not have to wait until we breathe our last in order to enjoy this reunion, this close encounter with God. The apostle Paul in 1 Corinthians 3 tells us that this wonderful future hope transforms the present:

> . . . since we have such a hope, we are very bold. We are not like Moses, who would put a veil over his face to prevent the Israelites from seeing the end of what was passing away . . . whenever anyone turns to the Lord, the veil is taken away. Now the Lord is the Spirit, and where the Spirit of the Lord is, there is freedom. And we all, who with unveiled faces contemplate the Lord's glory, are being transformed into his image with ever-increasing glory, which comes from the Lord, who is the Spirit.
>
> *2 Cor. 3:12–18*

One day we will see Jesus face to face and I look forward to that, home at last. But we don't have to just wait for that day because right now we have the firstfruits, a taster of this wonderful future. In John 14, Jesus told his disciples that although he was returning to his Father, he would not leave them without a 'Comforter',[15] an encourager. The Holy Spirit would come and he would be even closer to them, bringing the presence of Jesus even closer than he had been when on the earth – he would be in them, encouraging, assuring and transforming them from the inside out – and that is what Paul meant in the verses quoted. Our faces are unveiled and we are able to contemplate God's glory, his overwhelming, bright presence, in the face of Jesus Christ our Saviour. Paul then goes on to say that this changes everything, it affects the present. Remember:

> Therefore we do not lose heart. Though outwardly we are wasting away, yet inwardly we are being renewed day by day. For our light and momentary troubles are achieving for us an eternal glory that far outweighs them all. So we fix our eyes not on what is seen, but on what is unseen, since what is seen is temporary, but what is unseen is eternal.
>
> *2 Cor. 4:16–18*

With so much uncertainty, fear and sadness in the world, it is time for the people of God to be focused on Jesus, to contemplate him and his glory, and have encounters with him that transform us. This changes us, and if you think I am exaggerating, let me show you something quite astonishing. I mentioned Jesus' transfiguration earlier. The Greek word for transfiguration is *metamorpho*, from which we get our English word 'metamorphism', a word we use to refer to the transformation of a caterpillar into a beautiful butterfly. That Greek word occurs in only two other places in the New Testament and one of them is the verse quoted above, 2 Corinthians 3:18. It is worth repeating:

And we all, who with unveiled faces contemplate the Lord's glory, are being transformed [*metamorpho*] into his image with ever-increasing glory, which comes from the Lord, who is the Spirit.

The other is in Romans 12:2:

Do not conform to the pattern of this world, but be *transformed* by the renewing of your mind. Then you will be able to test and approve what God's will is – his good, pleasing and perfect will. (my emphasis)

In other words, when we as Christians take time to linger in the presence of the Lord, contemplating him and asking the Holy Spirit to open the eyes of our hearts, our inner being, to the beauty of Jesus, then we will be impacted and changed as we see something of his glory, and it is reflected in and through our lives right where we are.

We started this chapter in the book of Genesis where Adam and Eve enjoyed 'cool of the day' conversations with their Creator God, enjoying face-to-face encounters with him, and I conclude this chapter with words from the end of the story. The final chapters of the book of Revelation tell us of the future God has for us and all his creation, our future hope. Firstly, chapter 21 speaks of 'a new heaven and new earth', a beautiful remade world, the way it was always intended to be. But then chapter 22, the very last chapter in the Bible, points us to the very centre, the personal climax of our future hope, reassuring us that hope really does win:

No longer will there be any curse. The throne of God and of the Lamb will be in the city, and his servants will serve him. *They will see his face*, and his name will be on their foreheads. There will be no more night. They will not need the light of a lamp or the light of the sun, for the Lord God will give them light. And they will reign for ever and ever.

Rev. 22:3–5, my emphasis

What a wonderful future! What a glorious moment – our welcome home! It is important for us to have this expectation clear in our mind's eye, and with the Holy Spirit's help, to warm our hearts, because we are not yet home. We live in a broken world where suffering is still a reality. I have been encouraged to see several contemporary Christian songs on the theme of our future hope, focusing on our expectation of seeing our Saviour face to face. I quoted a song by Matt Redman at the opening of this chapter and I close with another by a good friend Olly Knight, entitled 'Longing':

> In our hearts there is a longing
> For our true eternal home
> Where we'll see our precious Saviour
> And we'll worship round the throne
>
> Oh the glory we will see
> Oh the wonder that awaits
>
> Jesus, how we long for You
> To see You face to face
> Dwelling with our Saviour
> Lost in wonder, love and praise
>
> There'll be no more grief or sadness
> You will wipe our tears away
> We'll be clothed in righteous garments
> When we meet You on that day[16]

11

Hope in the Face of Suffering

*When suffering sandblasts us to the core, the true stuff of which
we are made is revealed. Suffering lobs a hand-grenade into our
self-centredness, blasting our soul bare, so we can be better
bonded to the Saviour.*

Joni Eareckson Tada[1]

I am not a hero. Like most human beings, I like to avoid pain
at any cost. A surgeon friend of mine once took me on a tour
of the Royal College of Surgeons in London and in one of the
halls was displayed all the various implements and tools that
have been used in surgery over the centuries. I nearly passed
out. To this day, despite the fact that I have now had many
operations myself and scores of injections and implants and so
forth, I still close my eyes when the needles come out. As I say,
I am not a hero; like most of us, I prefer to avoid pain.

You may have heard Joni Eareckson Tada's story. At the age
of just seventeen, she broke her neck in a diving accident that
left her a quadriplegic, paralysed from the shoulders down.
Joni has suffered and continues to suffer pain far beyond what
I have suffered, and yet through it all she has not let go of
her hope in the goodness and kindness of God. Instead, as she
says in the quote above, her suffering has bonded her closer to
her Saviour.

But, you may well ask, why so much pain and over so many years? Was there not an easier way for her devotion to the Lord to grow? Let me be honest, there have been times when I have questioned God about our loss and my health: 'Why is this happening to us?' 'If you are God, a loving God, a God who is in control, why have you allowed this to happen?' And I had many compelling reasons to offer as to why God should have stepped in and healed our daughter – her young children needed her, as did her husband and many friends who valued her love, friendship and kindness. I understood something of Job's difficulty when he said to God: 'I cry to you for help and you do not answer me; I stand, and you only look at me.'[2] Job never did get to know the reason for all his suffering during his lifetime; instead, he was given a vision so magnificent that it caused all his questions to evaporate. He was given a vision of the overwhelming majesty of God, a vision that drew him in, bringing him closer to the Lord himself, and that was more valuable to him than all his losses and all his questions. In the climax to the story Job declares: 'My ears had heard of you but now my eyes have seen you.'[3] He had become 'better bonded' to his Lord.

The thought that an experience of God's presence and person could be better than enjoying a healthy, secure, fulfilled, provided-for life surrounded by loving friends or family might sound strange to our Western ears. We have been brought up in a culture that prizes strength and beauty, talent and self-sufficiency, and gives much time, attention and money to the grooming and nurturing of those attributes. The problem lies not so much in the inherent value of our health, abilities and gifts, as they can and should be seen as blessings from our Creator God; the problem lies in the fact that we quickly come to rely on what we consider to be our own resources and do life in our own strength. We become self-reliant with little need to look to God for help or hope. But that is not the way of the Christian disciple because we are looking in the wrong direction. Instead of growing in our knowledge and love of the Lord, learning to entrust our lives increasingly to him, relying on him at every turn, we end up looking to ourselves and our own resources to navigate life.

Certainly, when it came to my health and physical wellbeing, that was not an area that I had needed to trust God for; in fact, I quite prided myself on my fitness. In my younger years I had rowed for the school first eight and have a good selection of medals and pewter tankards to show for it. Later in life I kept fit by running regularly and cycling, and best of all, sailing! I saw no reason to doubt that I could expect a lengthy, ailment-free retirement. I am a very different person today. After more than twelve years of battling cancer, I am much more aware of my physical frailty, my total dependence on my heavenly Father for each day that I live, and the glaringly obvious truth that this life is short. And I long for the next. My perspective has changed and for that I am grateful. Yes, I too have, through the challenges of my health, become 'better bonded' to my Saviour, who I now long to be with. It has not been an easy or comfortable path to tread; in fact, as I write, I am recovering from yet another operation and feeling rather uncomfortable, but I am grateful for what Christ Jesus my Lord has done in me through this illness.

The apostle Paul gives us some helpful words on this subject, citing his own situation. He had what he called a 'thorn in [his] flesh'[4] that troubled him. He does not say exactly what it was but it sounds like a physical ailment, something that the enemy used to torment him, possibly tempting him to feel discouraged, frustrated or just physically pained. If you know or have known illness or physical challenges, you will identify with him. Whatever it was, Paul tells us that he pleaded with the Lord several times to take it away, to heal him. That is what we do when we are sick. We are not masochists who welcome pain, or Stoics who just suppress our feelings and soldier on. Scripture tells us to pray, believing for healing.[5] But, Paul continues, his 'thorn in [the] flesh' did not go away, he was not healed. Instead, God spoke to him, telling him, and us, that this situation, challenging though it was, brought an opportunity for God's power to be displayed in his life. You will recognize the familiar words:

> Three times I pleaded with the Lord to take it away from me. But he said to me, 'My grace is sufficient for you, for my power is made perfect in weakness.' Therefore I will boast all the more gladly about my weaknesses, so that Christ's power may rest on me. That is why, for Christ's sake, I delight in weaknesses, in insults, in hardships, in persecutions, in difficulties. For when I am weak, then I am strong.
>
> *2 Cor 12:8–10*

It is often when we feel weak, when we feel helpless on our own, that we learn to put our trust in the Lord and start to depend on him and find him to be everything we need and more. We have started to look in the right direction. Our perspective begins to change and we start to realize that the things we used to rely on and place our confidence in are actually quite feeble and unreliable in comparison. The physical health and strength of our bodies is limited and, I am sorry to have to tell you, starts to decline somewhere in your middle years. But now, looking in the right direction, towards the risen Lord Jesus, we begin to understand that this life with all its challenges is just the prelude to something far more wonderful, lasting and glorious!

Earlier in the same letter, Paul writes about this perspective of the Christian:

> Therefore we do not lose heart. Though outwardly we are wasting away, yet inwardly we are being renewed day by day. For our light and momentary troubles are achieving for us an eternal glory that far outweighs them all. So we fix our eyes not on what is seen, but on what is unseen, since what is seen is temporary, but what is unseen is eternal.
>
> *2 Cor. 4:16–18*

I know only too well that the trials and troubles that we face often seem to be far from 'light and momentary', yet the point Paul is making is that there is a comparison to be made. What he is saying is that our troubles or trials appear 'light and momentary' once we start to look in the right direction and compare them with the eternal, lasting, awesome 'weight of glory'[6] that those very trials and troubles are achieving for us! In other words, if you or I are experiencing trials that seem overwhelming, what we need is a greater, weightier awareness and anticipation of what lies ahead. We need to weight the scales with more future hope!

Before moving on, there are some lingering questions that Angie and I certainly had to grapple with concerning suffering. The first is one that quickly springs to mind when we have lost a loved one, namely – why does God heal some people and not others? Is it something to do with our faith, or lack of it? The Lord spoke to us about this one by leading us to an unexpected place in the book of Acts, chapter 12, to the account of Peter's miraculous escape from prison. It is a wonderful, dramatic story. Peter has been arrested and put in jail, chained to multiple guards (probably because his jail-breaking exploits were becoming legendary) awaiting trial. In the middle of the night a miracle takes place. An angel appears, flooding the cell with light, causing chains to fall off and prison doors to burst open such that Peter walks free! Wonderful! What an answer to prayer! But wait a minute, look back to the first two verses of that chapter. This is what it says: 'It was about this time that King Herod arrested some who belonged to the church, intending to persecute them. He had James, the brother of John, put to death with the sword' (Acts 12:1–2). This is awful; a disciple of Jesus put to death at the whim of a despotic king. But in the next verses we read the account of the miraculous deliverance of another disciple! Was it that God's people prayed with more faith for Peter than they had for James? I don't think so, because if you read the story, when Peter arrived at the house where the prayer meeting was taking place, although they were praying for his release, they didn't believe it could be him! And here is the interesting thing: Luke, who wrote Acts, doesn't even stop to explain or justify what has happened, as though it were unfair or strange. God is sovereign and works his good purposes for his glory.

The other question that troubled us was this. I have argued that God can and does use suffering for our good, to bring us to a greater dependence on and enjoyment of himself. But is not sickness and suffering evil? That raises the question – surely a good, loving God would not wish evil on his children, would he? If you have watched a loved one die from an awful disease, you may well have found yourself asking the question that most of us ask at such tragically painful moments: 'If you are God, a loving God, a God who is in control, why have you allowed this to happen?' How do we answer these questions?

Firstly, do I believe that God is in control, that he is sovereign over all? Yes, I do. Many verses in the Bible attest to that truth. Secondly, do I believe that God is loving? Again, yes, I believe that is what the Bible teaches. But how can both be true? If he is all powerful *and* loving, why does he allow painful things to happen to us? As Angie and I struggled with this seeming paradox, we came across a comment from D.A. Carson that we found helpful: 'It must be the case that God stands behind good and evil in somewhat different ways.'[7] He does not delight in evil; he hates it, but he uses things such as suffering and death in order to bring about something good, something beautiful that we will one day understand. Of course, being sovereign, he knows the end of the story – for which I thank God – whereas of course we, as yet, do not. An often-quoted Bible verse tells us: 'in all things God works for the good of those who love him, who have been called according to his purpose.'[8] In the words of Samwise quoted earlier, on regaining consciousness after the horrors he and Frodo went through in Mordor: 'Is everything sad going to come untrue?'[9] For the Christian, the answer is, 'Yes, it is!' And that gives me great encouragement. And hope.

There is an important link in the Bible between suffering and glory. They frequently go together, one leading to another. It was because of his awareness of the glory that lay ahead of him that Jesus was able to endure the cross![10] We have already seen that Paul understood that in some way, his and our suffering achieves, brings about, an eternal 'weight of glory', and it is as we catch a glimpse of this that our trials and troubles become less overwhelming. I am beginning to see that the great sadness that Angie and I have walked through with the sudden, horrible death of our daughter, Ali, will one day be turned into something very beautiful and Jesus-glorifying as we trust in the

One who has loved us and overcome death for us. Everything sad *is* going to come untrue when Jesus returns to wipe away every tear and make all things new.[11] Moreover, I have also found that I now live with a longing for that day! Instead of the coming of Jesus, or my going to be with him being a far-off, somewhat hazy event that I would rather not think about until I have to, my anticipation of Jesus' return to make all things new, or my death in the meantime, no longer hold any fear for me. Now, don't get me wrong, our lives are wonderful gifts from God and we seek to make the most of each day, living with joy and gratitude to God for all his goodness, but returning to the theme of pilgrims and settlers discussed earlier in the book, I have found that through both my own battle with cancer and the loss of our daughter, my attachment to life in this present, broken world has been weakened, and my longing for the next, strengthened.

Returning to Joni Eareckson Tada's words quoted at the start of this chapter and earlier in the book, I hope you are beginning to see how God is able to use those painful moments in our lives to bond us closer to our Saviour. Think of Jesus' disciple Peter and that painful moment when his failure, his betrayal of Jesus, dawned on him on hearing the cock crow. That must have been a rock-bottom moment for him, leaving him wondering if there was any future for him as a Jesus follower. After all his boasting of how he was ready to die with Jesus,[12] he had just denied him. Three times.[13] And yet it was on the back of that spectacular failure that Jesus spoke to dear Peter about his unchanging love for him, and the eyes of his heart were opened to the astonishing loving acceptance of his Saviour.[14] It was as a result of that painful experience that his life was transformed and he became 'better bonded' to his Saviour.

It is often in our vulnerable moments that we are most alert to and receptive of the extraordinary love of God towards us personally. The apostle Paul understood this when writing to Christians in Ephesus who were in danger of becoming discouraged on hearing of his imprisonment. Instead of discouragement, he prayed that they would be given power to grasp more of the expansive love of Christ for them.

> I pray that out of his glorious riches he may strengthen you with power through his Spirit in your inner being, so that Christ may dwell in your hearts through faith. And I pray that you, being rooted and established in love, may have power, together with all the Lord's holy people, to grasp how wide and long and high and deep is the love of Christ, and to know this love that surpasses knowledge – that you may be filled to the measure of all the fullness of God.
>
> *Eph. 3:16–19*

What wonderful words! And what a wonderful thing to pray for someone – that deep within them, in their heart of hearts, at the very core of their being they might know the living, loving presence of their Saviour and his overwhelming love for them, whatever the circumstances around them. Rather than praying for their outward circumstances to change, Paul prays for change in their inner being, for them to be anchored, held secure in God's loving grasp in such a way that outward circumstances would not throw them. Why? Because he knew the priority of the inner self over outward circumstances, the significance of things eternal over things temporal, and the importance of being bonded to the Saviour. This is the route to true and lasting riches, to maturity as a Christian. Speaking of the above passage of Scripture, Martyn Lloyd-Jones comments: 'It is undoubtedly one of the great mountain peaks in Scripture . . . if not the highest peak of all in the entire glorious range of Scripture truth and divine revelation . . . Here is the key to true Christian living.'[15]

We should not miss the point that these verses also tell us that we need help if we are to really get hold of the extent of Christ's love for us; we need power, the working of the Holy Spirit in us to enable us to grasp it. We cannot manufacture it or just educate ourselves into it. It was John Piper who, commentating on the apostle Paul's statement that we are 'temples of the Holy Spirit',[16] that the Holy Spirit resides in us, concluded that 'Christian living is supernatural or it is nothing',[17] and he is right; from start to finish, the Christian life is supernatural. It was the gracious initiative of God towards us when we were dead in our sins that brought about the start of our Christian life, and it is the gracious working of his indwelling empowering presence in us, often in the challenges and desperate moments of our lives, that causes priceless truths such as his love for us to go from brain to heart – to melt, comfort and transform us.

In the weeks following the death of our daughter I camped out in these verses, reading them, praying them, calling out to God in my sorrow, that he would open the eyes of my heart to comprehend his love in a way that would comfort and bless us. Yes, I read many articles and sermons on the subject of the sovereignty of God, but what I needed most of all was not convincing arguments or answers but the strengthening, reassuring richness of God's presence in my inner being. I needed to know the comfort that comes from grasping afresh the overwhelming love of Christ – his love for me, for Angie, and for our family, and so be 'better bonded' to him.

I have used the word 'comfort' several times in the last few sentences. Comfort is love expressed and received. Comfort speaks to the heart, not just the mind, and that is what Paul prayed for the Christians in Ephesus. He wanted them to know the love of God in their hearts, their inner beings – that is, in a way that goes beyond an intellectual understanding and warms their hearts. Angie and I were blessed to experience the comfort of God through the love and kindness shown us by friends and church family, but what we wanted most of all was that heart-felt love of Christ for us. You will have realized by now what an important part songs and worship play in our lives, especially in challenging moments, and I close this chapter with some words from another song written by our good friend Olly Knight that has been a great encouragement to Angie and myself following the loss of our daughter, Ali, and is often to be heard around our home. It is a song entitled 'God of All Comfort':

God of all comfort and God of all peace
God through our trials and God in our grief
My Rock and my Refuge brings rest to my soul
The Father of comfort is making me whole

God of all comfort and God of all grace
God in our sorrow and God in our pain
My Saviour shed tears over suffering and death
Jesus who comforts shares my lament

God of all comfort and God of all care
God in our questions and God through despair
My Healer draws near and His love I receive
The Spirit of comfort is dwelling in me

I will praise Your name, I will praise Your name
I will praise Your name, oh Lord
I will praise Your name, I will praise Your name,
I will praise Your name, O Lord[18]

12

Holding On to Hope

I wait for the LORD, my whole being waits,
and in his word I put my hope.
I wait for the Lord more than watchmen wait for the morning,
more than watchmen wait for the morning.

Israel, put your hope in the LORD,
for with the LORD is unfailing love
and with him is full redemption.

Ps. 130:5–7

A few hours ago I had the great joy of holding my newly born grandson, Jesse, in my arms. It was a very special moment. Less than a day old, this tiny little bundle of tissue and cells woven together so intricately made a very touching sight to behold. As I looked at his tiny features, eyes, nose, ears, those perfect little fingers, I was moved once again at the wonder of God-given life. The waiting was over. For my daughter-in-law, Natalie, it marked the end of nine long months of waiting, sometimes uncomfortable, occasionally anxious, but always expectant waiting.

The culture we live in does not encourage waiting. Gone are the days when one had to patiently save up to purchase a new television, refrigerator or whatever. Nowadays there are numerous ways to avoid the waiting and take delivery now, by using credit cards, taking out loans or running up debts. 'Why wait when you can have it now!' is an oft-repeated slogan of advertisers persuading us that we urgently need to make yet one more purchase. Now! This urgent impatience quickly spreads to other areas of life and we come to expect quick replies, instant access, speedy resolution to our problems. Instead of having to wait a couple of days for a letter to reach its destination, followed by another two or three days for a reply to reach us, an email can be sent around the world in seconds and a reply expected shortly after. Such a mindset can quickly lead not only to impatience and frustration if solutions do not come our way promptly, but also to weariness if we start to dance to the tune of the culture of 'now'. We live in a busy, urgent world where restlessness abounds and waiting does not come easily.

The Bible says a lot about waiting and resting because it speaks of an important part of the Christian life. It is a walk of faith, learning to trust God in the waiting when all the evidence around would seem to suggest that he is absent, uncaring or just unable to help. In the previous chapter I mentioned Joni Eareckson Tada's comment that the challenges of suffering can work in such a way in our lives that we become 'better bonded to the Saviour'. Interestingly, the word 'wait' that appears so often in the Bible does not mean the kind of waiting that we might do in a doctors' surgery or at a bus stop. In the Old Testament, the Hebrew word literally means 'to be bound to', and in the New Testament, the Greek word means 'to receive to oneself'. The idea, far from being a passive condition, is one of being bound to, holding on to. If I add that deeper sense to the verse quoted at the opening of this chapter it becomes, in my paraphrase:

I hold on to the Lord, I embrace and hold on to him with my whole being.

That sounds very deliberate and purposeful. Sometimes, such is the pain, the darkness of the moment, that all we can do is hold on to the Lord until the dawn breaks, the darkness lifts and we can sing again. This last week was our daughter, Ali's, birthday. She would have been 40. It was a day for remembering, for being grateful, yet feeling a sense of great loss; for weeping, for waiting, holding on to the Lord and the sure hope that we have a wonderful future hope beyond the grave. I don't know your story or the nature of your waiting. It could be deep sadness over the loss of a loved one. It could be loneliness or disappointment at the way life has treated you. Maybe you battle with depression and wonder how you can keep going. Let me encourage you by telling you that God does not abandon you at such times but is present and active, and although you might be tempted to doubt it, be reassured that God's Word is true, his character unchanging and he is able to perform a work of grace in your life through the process.

The apostle Paul was no stranger to difficulties and hardship. When under the scrutiny of the church at Corinth, he spoke candidly about the challenges that he had recently been subjected to and the effect that it had on him: 'We were so utterly burdened beyond our strength that we despaired of life itself.'[1] Despaired of life itself? The great apostle Paul? Yes, and he continues in that letter to tell of his thorn in the flesh that caused him real torment and which went unhealed, whatever physical ailment it was. It is widely thought that some in the church at Corinth considered themselves so spiritual that they deemed Paul not to be spiritual nor a very successful apostle because of his setbacks and difficulties. One of his purposes in writing this letter to the Corinthians was to explain to them that true spirituality is not about being strong and oblivious to the challenges of life, but rather in the midst of them, not being afraid to own one's weakness. It is about looking to the Lord Jesus and leaning on him, hearing the reassuring words: 'My grace is sufficient for you, for my power is made perfect in weakness.'[2] Speaking of his own situation, Paul goes on to say: 'Therefore I will boast all the more gladly of my weaknesses, so that the power of Christ may rest on me.'

What this means for us is that the Christian life is not always about being spared or delivered from difficult, dark moments, but rather seeing those challenging times as opportunities to intentionally turn to our heavenly Father. To cry out to him, or wait on him in silence, looking at his Word when we have no words, and then trusting him to come and supply the help, the healing, the grace and strength needed in the waiting. Trust is hope in the waiting. It means holding on to his promises instead of listening to lies and drifting into doubts. Paul speaks of a discovery of God's grace and power in his moments of weakness. Allow me to suggest how we too can make that discovery in our lives.

Firstly, let me encourage you by assuring you of God's compassion for his people who are suffering, enduring dark times, perhaps experiencing burnout. The children of Israel were slaves in Egypt on the treadmill of endless production, turning out bricks with no straw, for a culture with no end to its appetite to produce more. Into that tiresome, painful situation spoke the God of the burning bush: 'Let my people go.' There is a wonderful verse just before this where the Lord explains to Moses why he is intervening on behalf of his people:

> I have indeed seen the misery of my people in Egypt. I have heard them crying out because of their slave drivers, and I am concerned about their suffering. So I have come down to rescue them from the hand of the Egyptians and to bring them up out of that land

into a good and spacious land, a land flowing with milk and
honey . . .

Hear God's heart for his oppressed, weary people. He sees into
their heavy hearts, hears their silent cries, is moved with compassion, and is ready and willing to act on their behalf, to bring
them into a future that is good, brimming with hope and lavish
provision, where there is rest for their weary souls. This is, of
course, a wonderful prelude to the salvation that Jesus brought
us – taking on human flesh and coming down to rescue us by
dying on a cross for our sin and rising from the dead to give us
a promised future hope. The words of Jesus sound very similar:

> Come to me, all you who are weary and burdened, and I will give
> you rest. Take my yoke upon you and learn from me, for I am
> gentle and humble in heart, and you will find rest for your souls.
>
> *Matt. 11:28–29*

What wonderful, heartening words they are! Just as God, on
seeing the misery of his people slaving away in Egypt had great
compassion on them, so too he has compassion on you and
me. It was said of Jesus that when looking at the crowds that
appeared 'harassed and helpless', 'he had compassion on them',
that he felt deeply for them.[3] Oh, that we would learn to take
hold of that invitation and come to him in our dry or dark
moments. Our natural reaction is often the opposite, to as-
sume that we would not be worthy or welcome in such an
'unspiritual' condition. But those are just the moments when
we are most welcome and when we are most helped. The writer
of Hebrews, addressing believers who were discouraged and
tempted to go back to their old ways, puts it plainly. Having

just argued that Jesus knows very well what it is like to be human and is able to fully empathize with us, he writes:

> Let us then approach God's throne of grace with confidence, so that we may receive mercy and find grace to help us in our time of need.
>
> *Heb. 4:16*

Where are we coming when we turn to the Lord? To a 'throne where grace', undeserved love and favour, abounds. So how should we approach? With 'confidence', even when we are tempted to feel very inadequate and unworthy. What will we receive if we will make that approach? We will find our heavenly Father's 'mercy' and 'grace to help us'. And most importantly, when ought we do this? In 'our time of need', when hope is running low and help is sorely needed – what wonderful counsel with such rich consequence! This is what it means to wait upon the Lord. This is how we hold on to hope.

Secondly, I would encourage you by pointing out that we were never meant to live the Christian life in isolation. God's purpose in the world is to have a large family. The gospel is to be preached to every nation and people group so that men and women, young and old, might come to know Jesus as their Saviour and be gathered together as 'God's special possession',[4] 'a people that are his very own',[5] the bride for which Jesus is returning.[6] The Christian life is to be lived in the community of the church family. We read of the church in the New Testament that they 'devoted themselves . . . to fellowship'[7] and that they opened their homes to one another.[8]

The word 'fellowship' might sound rather old-fashioned and may for some bring to mind images of tea in the church hall, but it is in fact a word rich in meaning. It speaks of sharing a common life together, the life of the risen Christ! It was fellowship with him that made us Christians and it is fellowship with one another that strengthens and keeps us through the challenges of life. The local church, the fellowship of believers, is a means of God's grace, a channel through which God's grace comes to us in a variety of ways. Most obviously there is the coming together on the first day of the week to worship God and hear his Word proclaimed, as has been the practice of Christians since New Testament times.[9] But there are also ways that God's grace comes to our lives that continue beyond Sundays, through friendships, encouragement, generosity, acts of kindness as the church embraces the true sharing, the give and take of fellowship.

A few weeks ago, one of our church family spoke publicly of the transformation that had taken place in his life as a result of the love and acceptance that he had been shown. He spoke of 'the miracle of fellowship' that he had experienced. No wonder the writers of the New Testament wrote so often of the importance of loving one another, of unity in the church[10] and of not neglecting our meeting together regularly. This is, I believe, so important in light of the recent COVID-19 pandemic that disrupted church gatherings so extensively, that I will quote in full the encouragement that the writer of Hebrews gives us:

> And let us consider how we may spur one another on towards love and good deeds, not giving up meeting together, as some are in the habit of doing, but encouraging one another – and all the more as you see the Day approaching.
>
> *Heb. 10:24–25*

This verse suggests that when we gather together as the church, the called-out ones,[11] we are anticipating our future gathering together to the Lord at his coming. We are gathering together to him! What an inspiring thought to have in mind when wondering whether or not to go along on a Sunday morning! Gathering together as God's worshipping community to give attention to God's words and to partake in the giving and receiving of fellowship is vital for our mutual encouragement and wellbeing as Christians and we neglect it at our peril. Without that weekly reminder of who we are, to whom we belong and what our future holds, we can quickly slip back into the mindset of the culture around us, with all its restless striving and paralysing fears. God gave us Sabbath rest as an ongoing reminder of whose world this is and to alert us to the fact that if we do not orientate our lives towards him, honouring and enjoying his presence, we will find ourselves going against the grain of creation and exhaust ourselves in the process. How foolish it would be for us to regard this lightly, and casually exchange this wonderful provision for a shopping spree or a day at the beach.

One last word on Sabbath rest. In the same way that God rested on the seventh day, having completed his work, so Jesus has now become our Sabbath rest, as we read in Hebrews 4. Having done everything necessary for us to be redeemed and brought back to himself, he sat down at the right hand of the Father – he rested – and he invites us to stop our striving for God's acceptance and rest in that which he won for us by dying on the cross in our place. No more condemnation. No more staying at a distance because we feel unworthy. Accepted in the Lord Jesus!

In the following chapter we will look at the testimony of the first Christians, and see another important way in which God's grace and power can help strengthen and equip us in the challenges of life as we wait for his appearing.

I close this chapter where I began, with the psalmist's words, describing how he, in a dark place, waits for the Lord: 'I wait for the Lord more than watchmen wait for the morning, more than watchmen wait for the morning.'

What a dramatic picture this is, of a watchman on the city wall peering into the darkness for the first glimpse of a ray of light. It is often said that it is darkest just before the dawn; whether that is true or not I do not know, but certainly darkness is not a comfortable place to be. In the darkness we can see very little but can imagine much. It is a time when we can feel very alone, isolated, even fearful. Oh, what a difference those first rays of light make – suddenly we can begin to see again and hope rises because we know for certain that a new day is approaching. Dear reader, if you find yourself in a dark, lonely place, I want you to know that in these challenging, often dark days, the sun – or perhaps I should say the Son – has risen! Jesus is alive and the light of his gracious, loving presence is available to shine into your darkness and will one day fill the whole cosmos! Listen to Zechariah's song, predicting the coming of Jesus:

> because of the tender mercy of our God,
> by which the rising sun will come to us from heaven
> to shine on those living in darkness
> and in the shadow of death,
> to guide our feet into the path of peace.

Luke 1:78–79

13

Hope That Transforms Life

The thing that was so obvious about the New Testament Christians,
as seen in Acts 2 or anywhere else, was their spirit of joy and of hap-
piness and assurance, their confidence; they were so certain, that they
were ready to be thrown to the lions in the arena or put to death.

Dr Martyn Lloyd-Jones[1]

When you read stories in the New Testament of Christians
singing in prison, counting beatings a privilege and being put
to death for their faith,[2] do you ever wonder how they were
able to do that, or how you would cope? For first-century followers of Jesus, this was a very real prospect and many did
become martyrs. In some parts of the world that is still the
case – and is becoming more prevalent.

How is it possible to sing and count beatings a privilege?
Were these disciples so unlike us? Were they super-Christians?
No, I don't think they were. Silas was not an apostle yet we
find him singing while imprisoned with Paul after having been
stripped and beaten with rods.[3] Then there was Stephen, the
first Christian martyr; he had just been given the lowly task
of waiting on tables before being falsely accused and stoned to
death, yet he faced death radiantly.[4] And if you read the New
Testament letters, you will discover that they were written to

real people in real churches; you will find that they faced temptations just as we do, failing at times, also just as we do. So, what made the difference such that they were able to endure persecution with a joyful disposition and even face martyrdom? Let me answer by using an illustration.

I am quite keen on sport and in particular, football. My fondness for the game goes back to my childhood when, living in London, I used to make the short journey to Stamford Bridge with a friend to watch Chelsea play. But perhaps my fondest memory is that of Saturday evenings watching *Match of the Day* with my father. It became something of a ritual in our household, just he and I comfortably installed in front of the TV for an enjoyable hour or so, watching the day's matches. (Actually, I went on to work on the *Match of the Day* programme years later in my BBC days, but that's another story.) What made those Saturday evenings so enjoyable was not just the good company, but the fact that we already knew the results because the games had been played several hours earlier. That meant that instead of sitting on the edge of our chairs in tense anticipation of what might happen, we could relax, sit back and enjoy the game, because we knew the result in advance. If we knew that our team would win, we could even watch them go a goal or two down, knowing that all would come good before the end of the match. Similarly, I believe that it was their absolute confidence in how the story of their lives would conclude that enabled those first Christians to endure difficult, painful times with poise and even joy. They knew that they had a hope that wins, and the same can be true for us.

Peter, disciple of Jesus, wrote a letter to Christians who were facing a very real threat of persecution. Writing at the time when Nero was emperor, Christians were already becoming targets for hatred and abuse and indeed Peter himself would shortly be martyred for his faith. In the course of his letter, his first epistle, he refers to suffering at least fifteen times and even alerts his readers to a fiery trial that is breaking out against Christians. You might therefore expect the tone of his letter to be subdued, extending sympathy and consolation or compassion. But no! The letter is brimming with joy! Right there alongside acknowledgement of their trials and suffering there are some of the most joyful words in the New Testament:

> Praise be to the God and Father of our Lord Jesus Christ! In his great mercy he has given us new birth into a living hope through the resurrection of Jesus Christ from the dead, and into an inheritance that can never perish, spoil or fade. This inheritance is kept in heaven for you, who through faith are shielded by God's power until the coming of the salvation that is ready to be revealed in the last time. In all this you greatly rejoice, though now for a little while you may have had to suffer grief in all kinds of trials. These have come so that the proven genuineness of your faith – of greater worth than gold, which perishes even though refined by fire – may result in praise, glory and honour when Jesus Christ is revealed. Though you have not seen him, you love him; and even though you do not see him now, you believe in him and are filled with an inexpressible and glorious joy . . .
>
> *1 Pet. 1:3–8*

What is the reason for this joy? Where does it come from? Because if ever there is a time we need joy in our lives, it is when we are suffering, facing painful situations. It is widely agreed that 'hope' is the keynote of this letter; in fact, Peter has already brought up the subject of hope in the opening verses quoted above, and you may have noticed that he refers to it as a '*living* hope'[5] or as J.B. Phillips translates it: 'we have been born again into a life full of hope'.[6] In other words, instead of it being a hope that is lodged in the future that will pay dividends one day, this is a hope that is active, that makes a difference *now*! It is a hope that brings the joy of heaven right where we need it, into the context of our suffering. Author Wayne Grudem paraphrases verse 8 above as follows:

> 'joy that has been infused with heavenly glory and that still possesses the radiance of that glory'. It is thus joy that results from being in the presence of God himself, and joy that even now partakes of the character of heaven. It is the joy of heaven before heaven, experienced now in fellowship with the unseen Christ.[7]

So it is the joy of heaven before heaven! A taster, a down payment of our inheritance just when we need it! And this the fruit, the outflow of our relationship with Jesus, because as we have already seen, he is the joy of heaven. This is what enabled those first-century Christians to endure hardship, to sing in prison – their spirit of joy and of happiness!

I cannot emphasize enough the important part that praise, worship and singing have played in my journey as a Christian, especially through the years of my battle with cancer. It really is true that 'the joy of the LORD is [our] strength'.[8] It has been my experience so often, sometimes in the most painful and challenging moments, to know a wonderful transformation the moment I falteringly start to worship Jesus in song. It might just be a simple refrain. It's not that I am particularly musical, because I don't think I am; rather, it is the spiritual significance of our worship. There have been so many instances when I have felt downcast or in pain and have slipped up to my study in the loft and just begun to worship Jesus with a simple, sometimes hardly audible refrain and found my mood lifted as the joy of the Lord warms my heart. Why is praising and worshipping with song so important? Put simply, it is because this is what we were made for – to know, worship and enjoy God. All of creation was made for the glory of God, to reflect something of his beauty, his majesty, and point towards him. 'The heavens declare the glory of God', the psalmist tells us in Psalm 19, 'Day after day they pour forth speech', but out of all creation only humankind can express his beauty, majesty – his glory – with heartfelt wonder, love and adoration.

The Bible is full of songs and singing and, of course, there is a songbook in the middle – the book of Psalms. Israel's was a singing faith . . . in the first instance out of gratitude for God's intervention and help on their behalf, such as when he had delivered them out of Egypt. But Israel also sang in celebration of God's attributes, his splendour, his goodness, his perfections, who he is, because they knew him, albeit in part, and they enjoyed knowing him, and singing gives expression to joy. The temple was full of joyful music and song. There were choirs of singers, musicians too, on duty permanently to be ready to minister to the Lord, such was the importance of worship and singing in Israel.[9] When we come into the New Testament, the joy and singing continues.

There are countless encouragements throughout the Bible urging us to sing out the praises of God:

> Let the peoples praise you, O God;
> let all the peoples praise you!
> Let the nations be glad and sing for joy,
> for you judge the peoples with equity
> and guide the nations upon earth.
> *Selah*
> Let the peoples praise you, O God;
> let all the peoples praise you!

Ps. 67:3–5 (ESV)

There are even hints that the creation around us has a part to play in praising God: 'Let the sea roar, and all that fills it; the world and those who dwell in it! Let the rivers clap their hands; let the hills sing for joy together'[10] – and that at the dawn of creation the stars joined in with the angels in shouting out for joy.[11] Is this merely poetic language? I am not so sure. The apostle Paul tells us that all creation is groaning, waiting for God's new creation to come into view.[12] Could it be that in some way, all of creation will somehow resound to the praise of God?

There is an enchanting scene in the first of C.S. Lewis's Chronicles of Narnia when the founding of Narnia is described:

> In the darkness something was happening at last. A voice had begun to sing . . . Then two wonders happened at the same moment. One was that the voice was suddenly joined by other voices; more voices than you could possibly count . . . The second wonder was that the blackness overhead, all at once, was blazing with stars . . . If you had seen it and heard it, you would have felt quite certain that it was the stars themselves which were singing, and that it was the First Voice, the deep one, which had made them sing.[13]

The singer, of course, turns out to be a Lion and as he sang, pacing to and fro, grass and valleys, trees and flowers, moles, rabbits and all kinds of creatures, even elephants appeared!

But I digress. It is us, humankind, made in the image of God, who are uniquely called to sing the praises of God. Yes, we can worship God silently and there is a sense in which the whole of our lives, actions, words and thoughts are to be part of our offering of worship to the Lord, but just as our prayers become more personal and focused when expressed in audible words (and we are less likely to drift off into musings, even sleep!), so too with our worship. When we sing our praises and our worship to God, it is as though a greater part of us becomes involved. Instead of just our minds, our cognitive self, when singing we are giving expression to our inner being, our emotions, our affections, our soul.

I think everybody knows this to be true – that singing gives expression to and heightens our affections. Small children, when happy and excited, will often overflow by humming a little tune, and lovers have always known the power of a love song sung to their beloved. But for the Christian, there is something else that happens when we sing our worship to Jesus. You may recall that when Jesus was encouraging his disciples before going to the cross, in the chapters in John known as the Upper Room Discourse, he said that he would not leave them like abandoned orphans but that he would send 'another Comforter', the Holy Spirit, and that he would be in them.[14] He went on to say that the Holy Spirit's task would be that of glorifying Jesus,[15] that is, lifting up, elevating, making much of him. So as Christians with the Holy Spirit living in us, the moment we begin to declare, to sing out our love and worship to Jesus, the Holy Spirit within us rises up, strengthening our sometimes feeble efforts and making Jesus more real and precious to us. It is as though as we start to worship the Holy Spirit says, 'You are glorifying Jesus! That is what I do, so let's do this together!' and the result is that we are encouraged, and blessed disproportionately to our stuttering efforts.

This discovery has made such a difference in my life, especially when walking through difficult, painful moments. As well as encouraging and helping me when experiencing physical pain, there have also been times when I have felt deep sorrow and sadness at the loss of our daughter, and yet even while the tears were still flowing, by opening my mouth and expressing my devotion to the Lord in song, I have experienced his strengthening, loving comfort flooding my soul and giving me joy.

I began this chapter by quoting Martyn Lloyd-Jones about the 'spirit of joy . . . happiness and assurance' of New Testament Christians and how it enabled them to face and endure persecution. We then looked at the letter that Peter wrote to Christians who were suffering under Emperor Nero's purge of Christians, shortly before Peter himself was put to death, and were perhaps surprised to hear Peter tell us that these dear people were 'filled with an inexpressible and glorious joy'.[16] Were they special people? No, Peter does not even know their names, referring to them as 'strangers scattered [abroad]'.[17] They were ordinary men and women who were certain about their future hope and were in fact enjoying something of the joy of heaven before heaven, as the result of the presence of the Holy Spirit in their lives.

Martyn Lloyd-Jones concludes:

God started the Christian church by pouring down his Spirit upon them. So the New Testament Church is a church that is baptised with the Spirit. And all the teaching of the New Testament assumes that . . . The apostle Peter knew that these people, having been baptised with the Spirit, were filled with a joy unspeakable, and full of glory. He, far from saying that it was exceptional, takes it as the standard and the norm.[18]

True to his word, Jesus had not left his followers as sad, forsaken orphans but had sent the Comforter, the Holy Spirit, to encourage, fill with joy and strengthen for the journey. Spoken of by Jesus as 'another *Comforter*',[19] with the promise that he will be with and in the disciples, the Holy Spirit is described as one who would in many regards take the place that Jesus had played in their lives and glorify him to them, as we saw above. In fact, Jesus went so far as to say that it was to the disciples' 'advantage' that he was to leave them because then the Comforter, the Holy Spirit, would come to help them and be with them forever.[20] God's empowering presence within them, presenting Jesus to them! That was the source of those first Christians' joy and can be ours too.

I will be honest with you – my relationship with Jesus has not always been like that. I was born into a loving Christian home, but although I believed in God, I knew little about a relationship with Jesus. In my teens I went to hear Billy Graham preach when he came to Earls Court, London in the mid-1960s, was deeply moved and responded to the call to give my life to Christ. I went forward and prayed the prayer of faith with real conviction. But I still didn't have the kind of joy-filled knowledge of Jesus that the apostle Peter speaks of. Yes, I was a Christian, but I wasn't a very confident, assured or joyful one and I can't say that I was a very consistent or victorious follower of Jesus. Then one Sunday I found myself surrounded by Christians who clearly had a far more intimate and joy-filled relationship with Jesus than I thought possible. I had gone to a church in central London, not because I was seeking a deeper walk with the Lord, but because I was seeking the company of a girl I rather liked who went there! I was struck by what I witnessed – people of all ages not just singing hymns in the way I was used to, but obviously expressing heartfelt devotion and yes, joy, as they sang! This was most unusual – especially back then, around 1970, you just did not do that in church. I was fascinated; these people were excited about their faith and they spoke openly about Jesus, not in the embarrassed way that I was used to.

As the weeks went by, I started to hear about the Holy Spirit and the gifts and joy that he gives, and that seemed to be the reason behind what I saw in these people. It quickly became obvious to me that if it is true the Holy Spirit wishes to fill the lives of believers with joy and spiritual gifts, so as to encourage them and make them more effective in their Christian lives, and if indeed Jesus promised this for all his followers, why would I not want this? I was tired of being ashamed of my faith, desperately hoping that no one would ask me on a Monday morning what I had done on Sunday, in case I had to own up to being a churchgoer. And so I became thirsty for what I saw in others and read about in Scripture; wonderful promises about God pouring out his Spirit on all people, about the coming of the Spirit on the disciples on the Day of Pentecost and the transformation that happened in them. Again and again I read of this wonderful, joy-filled, gift-giving experience of those first Christians – at Samaria, in the house of Cornelius, in Ephesus[21] – and I longed for it. And so I took every opportunity to be prayed for.

At first nothing much happened, but that just made me more thirsty, more determined to take Jesus at his word and go after all that he has for me. Then one evening, almost fifty years ago now, in the context of a worship meeting, I was prayed for and encouraged to speak out my heartfelt devotion and longing to know more of Jesus, and as I did so, I found myself singing and overwhelmed with a sense of the knowledge of his nearness and love for me in a way that I had never known before. It was a life-changing moment, giving me a joy and a confidence as a Christian that I did not previously have.

There is something else about the first Christians that is important. There has been a recurring tendency among God's people to lose sight of who they are, who they belong to. Peter does not want this to happen to his readers. If we go back to 1 Peter 1:1, we read that they are 'God's elect, exiles, scattered throughout the provinces of Pontus, Galatia, Cappadocia, Asia and Bithynia'. That word 'exiles' is important. The Greek word for exile primarily means temporary residents, foreigners who settle temporarily in a place without any intention of living there permanently. Peter is making the point that just like God's people in the Old Testament who were scattered during the time of the Babylonian Exile, so too these first-century Christians were living away from their true home. Just as we read in the book of Daniel that Daniel and his friends had to resolve to hold on to their true identity as Jews and not take on the diets, dealings and deities of the Babylonians around them, so too as followers of Jesus we must not settle and lose sight of who we belong to and where our true home is. The exiles lived and longed for their homeland, thinking and singing of it often, as we see in Psalm 137:1: 'By the rivers of Babylon we sat and wept when we remembered Zion.'

In the same way, Peter reminds his readers that they too are a pilgrim people, temporary residents living with an expectation of an 'inheritance . . . kept in heaven'.[22] This theme of Christians being a journeying people living with the tension of residing as exiles while longing for their true homeland resonates throughout the New Testament.

Do not store up for yourselves treasures on earth, where moths and vermin destroy, and where thieves break in and steal. But store up for yourselves treasures in heaven, where moths and vermin do not destroy, and where thieves do not break in and steal. For where your treasure is, there your heart will be also.

Matt. 6:19–21

Jesus' warning is clear. There is a danger, a tension of conflicting interests competing for our hearts. Will our hearts be set on treasure in heaven or treasure on earth? It cannot be both. Paul also uses this two- world tension in Colossians 3:1–2: 'Since, then, you have been raised with Christ, set your hearts on things above, where Christ is, seated at the right hand of God. Set your minds on things above, not on earthly things.' To the Philippian Christians he laments:

> For, as I have often told you before and now tell you again even with tears, many live as enemies of the cross of Christ. Their destiny is destruction, their god is their stomach, and their glory is in their shame. Their mind is set on earthly things. But our citizenship is in heaven. And we eagerly await a Saviour from there, the Lord Jesus Christ . . .
>
> *Phil. 3:18–20*

It was precisely because Peter's readers were living as resident exiles, like Daniel years before, loving and longing for their true heavenly inheritance, that they had such joy on the journey. They were receiving a taster ahead of time by the Spirit!

The same can be said of the African-American slaves of the American South. Labouring in harsh conditions in the cotton fields, they knew only too well where their home and treasure was and they sang songs celebrating it, giving rise to what we know as Spirituals. The same is true of Christians throughout history. When their treasure is clearly heaven-focused then their joy on earth soars, but when they lose sight of their true identity and start to live as though this world is the only home they will ever have, then they exchange their joy-filled future hope for the cares and worries that this world trades in.

14

Living Life with Heaven's Perspective

God gave us Revelation not to tickle our fancy,
but to strengthen our hearts.

Vern Poythress[1]

If we are to make sense of our lives and the world around us, we all need to see ourselves and the events of our lives as part of a narrative, a story. That story might be something like studying and working hard in life in order to become successful, or travelling the world to broaden our horizons and experiences, or finding the right partner and raising and supporting a family. But what happens if the career collapses, or the success becomes hollow, or the adventure leaves us lonely, or the family fractures? Looking beyond our own circumstances, what happens if the world around us becomes unstable through regime change, terrorism or global warming? And what happens to the story of our lives if sickness strikes, or when we face the end of our days on earth? The answer is that we become fearful or disillusioned, or maybe just sad and cynical because hope is lost. What we need is a bigger story, one that offers a bigger, more substantial and lasting hope.

Is there a story, in which our lives and the happenings in the world around us are framed, that is big enough not just to make sense of our own lives, but also make sense of the history and happenings in the world? Yes, there is, and the Bible tells us that story. In Chapter Ten, we looked at the Bible narrative from a personal perspective and saw that we were always intended to enjoy a face-to-face relationship with the God who made us and delights in us. In this chapter, we will look at God's purpose and plan for the whole of his creation.

In recent years, I have found myself drawn to astronomy. I don't know as much about it as I would like, but that doesn't prevent me from being captivated by the sheer scale and magnificence of the universe that surrounds us. I very much enjoy bringing my grandchildren up to my study in the loft on a clear evening to look at the night sky through my telescope. It never fails to adjust my thinking when I consider the vastness of the universe. I am awed and made to feel very small, and as a Christian, astonished that the one who created it with loving purpose, who brought everything into being by his 'powerful word',[2] set every star in place, every planet in its orbit, knows me personally by name. Of course, to many, what I have just written is hugely presumptuous, naïve and unbelievable. They choose instead to believe that all that can be seen and touched – themselves included – is actually the chance coming together of atoms and molecules and therefore of no lasting significance or meaning.

I was recently interested to discover that Matt Redman, best known for his songs and songwriting, is also interested in astronomy. He has written a wonderfully illustrated book entitled *Indescribable: Encountering the Glory of God in the Beauty of the Universe* with page after page of magnificent pictures of the cosmos. In the book he writes the following:

We surge upward in our spacecraft and gaze upward with our telescopes because we were made for something more. For every heart with the grace to recognize it, we soon find ourselves encountering the glory of God in the beauty of the universe.[3]

The book of Genesis tells of our beginnings when God 'created the heavens and the earth',[4] declaring it to be good. Everything changed as a result of humankind's rebellion against God, leaving humanity estranged from him, and the world out of harmony. Sin entered the world, and is plain to see. Although the world continues to be beautiful, like humankind, it is less so than originally intended. It is a beautiful ruin. But when God set out to redeem and restore humankind, the pinnacle of his creation, back to his intended relationship with their creator, his work of restoration was not limited to humanity. The story unfolding throughout the Bible from Genesis to Revelation tells of God's overarching plan of redemption, the restoration of all of creation; the book of Revelation shows us what is in store as we approach the conclusion of history, 'his story'.

For many, Revelation remains a closed book because it seems to be so different to the rest of the Bible and is not straightforward to understand. For others, it is viewed rather like a jigsaw puzzle but without the picture on the box to show how it all fits together, and so in trying to piece it all together they come up with all sorts of conflicting scenarios that are then endlessly argued about. Let me say that I believe that Revelation is a book to be understood – that is the whole point of the last book in the Bible, and revelation in general. Revelation is to reveal! The Greek word *apocalupto*, from which we get our English word 'apocalypse', means to uncover, to draw back the curtain. Can the book of Revelation be understood? In my view, absolutely. And the headline is that God wins! In fact, the whole purpose of the book is to remind God's people of the fact that they have a wonderful future hope that is secure.

God gave John, the disciple of Jesus, a series of visions depicting the time of waiting that Christians must live through until Jesus returns, at a time when widespread persecution was breaking out against the church (something that has continued in the world ever since). Many Christians were being put to death and John himself was taken forcibly from his home in Ephesus and exiled on the island of Patmos. It was there that God gave him these visions to alert, encourage and equip the Christians in his day, and in each generation since, by giving them heaven's perspective on the things that happen in the world around us while we wait for the decisive day when Jesus returns. As well as the warnings of difficulties ahead, there are some wonderful encouragements and words of reassurance for us to hear. I don't expect this chapter to answer all the questions you have about Revelation, that will have to wait for another book, but I do aim to open your eyes to see what is happening in the world from heaven's perspective so as to encourage your heart and strengthen your hope.

Revelation is a book to be *seen*. It is, for the large part, a vision or series of visions, and visions need to be seen and inter-preted. The phrase 'I saw' occurs again and again throughout the book. What is needed, amid all the confusion that people often have about the book of Revelation, is a strategy for see-ing; so where should we look to find the correct interpretation of the visions that John saw? Stating the obvious, Revelation is the last book in the Bible! What I mean is that in it, John, under the Holy Spirit's guidance, draws together many strands of biblical images and expectations drawn from throughout Scripture, bringing them to fulfilment here in Revelation. John's mind is saturated in Bible truths and he quotes the Old Testament more than 500 times, drawing widely from Genesis through to the Prophets. So, we can say that the Revelation only makes sense in the light of the whole of the Bible and that's where we should look when seeking to interpret symbols and prophecies – not science fiction! For instance, we read of plagues and locusts and so forth, and if we know our Bibles that will remind us of the Exodus when God brought his people out of captivity in Egypt and in to the Promised Land. John is telling us that there is another, glorious exodus ahead when God will bring his people into a new, perfect promised land. Most importantly, the book of Revelation shows us Jesus Christ at the centre. Right from the start, we are introduced to Jesus Christ, no more veiled by his humanity as he was when walking this earth. Now he is all glory! He is awesome, dazzling, so much so that John falls down:

> When I saw him, I fell at his feet as though dead. Then he placed his right hand on me and said: 'Do not be afraid. I am the First and the Last.'
>
> *Rev. 1:17*

The first thing that Christians need in challenging moments when their lives and the world around them seem to be falling apart, is a big vision of Jesus, King Jesus, the one who reigns supreme. Nations may rage and wage war, but Jesus reigns supreme, holding us, history and the universe in his hands.

In this first heavenly vision, John sees something that would have been very encouraging for the churches that he loved and served, but had been separated from. Jesus, the risen, ascended, all-powerful one, not only has things to say to the churches; he sees them as golden lampstands and is walking among them. In his book *A People Prepared*, Terry Virgo draws out the wonderful truths seen in this vision:

> 'Christ loved the church and gave himself up for her' (Eph 5:25). She is his special delight in all the universe. She is his joy, his preoccupation, his passion, his darling bride. In all creation one thing

fills the heart of Christ – his beloved church. We need to rediscover the incredible value and significance of the local church in
God's plan and perspective. She is not to be ignored and despised;
she is to be honoured and cherished. Each lampstand is not plastic
but golden – of peerless worth to Christ.[5]

The next vision John sees is of a scroll representing the story
of history and the future. It is sealed closed with seven seals,
and in Revelation 5:2 an angel cries out 'Who is worthy to
break the seals and open the scroll?' (Who controls the course
of history? Who knows what the future holds for the world and
its inhabitants?) In verse 4 we read that John 'wept and wept'
because it seemed that no one knew or was able to tell of what
might happen; the future of the world was out of control. Then
comes the most significant announcement in the whole of the
book of Revelation. The course of world history is not out of
control, spiralling to destruction! John tells us the reason:

> Then I saw a Lamb, looking as if it had been slain, standing at
> the centre of the throne . . . He went and took the scroll from
> the right hand of him who sat on the throne. And when he had
> taken it, the four living creatures and the twenty-four elders fell
> down before the Lamb. Each one had a harp and they were hold-
> ing golden bowls full of incense, which are the prayers of God's
> people. And they sang a new song, saying: 'You are worthy to
> take the scroll and to open its seals, because you were slain, and
> with your blood you purchased for God persons from every tribe
> and language and people and nation. You have made them to be
> a kingdom and priests to serve our God, and they will reign on
> the earth.'

Rev. 5:6–10

King Jesus is the one who has triumphed over sin and death, over all principalities and powers by his death and resurrection! He is the one who will have the final word about our future, and his kingdom will include people from 'every tribe and language . . . and nation'. What is more, they will reign '*on the earth*'[6] – there is a future, not just for his people, but for the world that he created. Before we reach the account of that day when Jesus returns to make all things new, John is given further visions; a vision of trumpets, telling of warnings that will sound out across the world just as God gave Pharaoh signs in the days before the Exodus. A vision of bowls of wrath, judgements coming on the earth; of a battle in the heavenlies and a tale of two cities, God's city Jerusalem and humanity's city, given the name Babylon; one destined for destruction, the other for a wonderful, glorious future, and it is to that we now turn.

With chapter 21 we come to the climax of the Bible, the conclusion to which all that goes before has been pointing. With Satan, sin and death all dealt with, the way is open for all to be restored to its former glory; in fact, to be made even more glorious, and lasting. In just one verse, verse 1, John tells us that he saw 'a new heaven and a new earth' because the 'first heaven and the first earth had passed away'. But his attention does not linger on this new creation to describe to us what it looked like because it is drawn to something even more stunning. Enough to say that if the first heavens and earth were largely stunningly beautiful then the new will be even more so. Make no mistake, this will be no makeover or repair of the old world any more than our resurrected, physical bodies will be patched up versions of our old bodies, and for that I am eternally grateful! John tells us that the one seated on the throne declares that he is making all things new.[7] In 1 Corinthians 15 the apostle Paul says much the same thing in verses often read at funerals: not only will our resurrected bodies have a 'splendour' about them, they will also be 'imperishable'.[8] But John's attention quickly moves on to describe something even more glorious, and it is a wedding! God's people, his inheritance, the precious company of the redeemed for whom Jesus died, are now seen as his beautiful bride, chosen and much loved! Jesus' first miracle when on earth took place at a wedding where he turned water into wine, as we read in John 2. Could it be that on that occasion John saw in his mind's eye the wedding feast that lay ahead? This was what he saw that arrested his attention, that was even more stunning than the new earth! An angel summoned him:

> 'Come, I will show you the bride, the wife of the Lamb.' And he carried me away in the Spirit to a mountain great and high, and showed me the Holy City, Jerusalem, coming down out of heaven from God. It shone with the glory of God, and its brilliance was like that of a very precious jewel, like a jasper, clear as crystal.
>
> *Rev. 21:9–11*

The whole point of a hope for something attractive in the future is that contemplating it gives us pleasure in the present. Part of the enjoyment of a planned holiday somewhere special is the anticipation that we enjoy while we wait. Our imaginations get to work, looking at the travel brochures and filling in the gaps with attractive possibilities. When it comes to our future hope it is absolutely appropriate that we do think about it and imagine what it might be like. We know that it will involve a physical existence, that we will enjoy food and drink – a feast, in fact. Jesus made a point of eating food when he appeared to his disciples after he rose from the dead. We know too that we will recognize and know one another just as the disciples recognized the risen Jesus, although it did require a second look – no weakness, wear and tear of the years, no disease nor deformity. All made new now. Will there be animals, cats and dogs? What about wild animals? Will they become vegetarian if they no longer hunt for prey? Enough to say that it will be stunningly beautiful, as on the first days of creation; Eden restored, made new, and all in glorious harmony, a symphony of praise and adoration that is focused on the one who brought about this unity to all things in heaven and on earth, as we see in Ephesians 1:10. Jesus, the Lamb that was slain, now all glory.

John's eyes are drawn to the focus, the centrepiece of this new creation – a love scene, a long-awaited reunion, a marriage. Just as the high point of the first creation was humankind, God's image-bearers, whose creation on day six caused God to observe that what he had made was 'very good',[9] so with the new creation. The imagery has changed from a bride to a vast city, the redeemed from every age, nation, peoples and tongue: the church. In the first Eden, Adam was commissioned to 'subdue the earth' and fill it,[10] as God's image-bearer, for God's glory, but because of humankind's rebellion it became instead a testament to humanity's rebellion and sinfulness. However, now what John sees is a vast city of people, all made perfectly righteous by the second Adam, Christ Jesus, and shining with the brilliance of his glory. John sees an angel measuring this huge city; it is shaped like a cube, about 1,400 miles long, wide and high! What is the significance of this? The inner sanctuary of the temple was cubic in shape, about 60ft in each direction, and that was where God's presence dwelt. God's presence is no longer confined – his dwelling place, his temple, is now his redeemed people filling the whole of creation. What the first Adam failed to do, the Second Adam has brought about through his death and resurrection, all for his glory! The church, the bride, the dwelling place of God, filling the whole earth with the glory of God. And somehow, in those moments, all the pains and the tears, the sorrow and losses, the heartache and the crosses, instead of being forgotten will somehow be transformed into objects of dazzling beauty, very precious jewels, adorning the bride for her Husband – seen and cherished.

The book of Revelation has not been given us to ignore or to amuse us, but rather to give us heaven's perspective on the happenings in the world around us. It assures us that God is sovereign, that he will have the last word and that the church, for which Jesus gave his life, is of greater worth and significance than we can imagine. For us as Christians this is the hope-filled perspective with which we are to live our lives. This is the story of which we are a part – a story so bold, so certain and so abounding in hope that it cannot be overwhelmed or diminished by anything this life throws at it. I close this chapter with a helpful reminder from scholar and pastor John Piper:

> The church of Jesus Christ is the most important institution in the world. The assembly of the redeemed, the company of the saints, the children of God are more significant in world history than any other group, organization, or nation. The United States of America compares to the church of Jesus Christ like a speck of dust compares to the sun. The drama of international relations compares to the mission of the church like a kindergarten riddle compares to Hamlet or King Lear. And all pomp of May Day in Red Square and the pageantry of New Year's in Pasadena fade into a formless grey against the splendor of the bride of Christ. Take heed how you judge. Things are not what they seem.[11]

15

Joy on the Journey

The fight to which we have been called is not an easy fight. We are touching the very centre of the devil's power and kingdom . . . No one is of much use who does not truly want to learn what it means to pray and listen and definitely choose the life that is hid with Christ in God. Keep close, keep close . . . walk with him as with a visible Companion, from dawn through all the hours till you go to sleep at night.

Amy Carmichael[1]

I have to confess to being a people watcher. If I am at an airport, I can't resist looking at the people around me, wondering where they are from and where they are going. You can tell a lot about people by the way they walk. Regular travellers make their way with a relaxed ease because they have done this so often, whereas those on an unfamiliar adventure look hesitant and anxious, trying to read the signs to direct them on their way. There are those who look bright and happy, possibly exhilarated at the thought of a holiday in the sun or a happy reunion ahead, while others look exhausted from their journey, heads bowed, maybe even asleep, leaning on their luggage. As Christians we have an astonishing destination and a wonderful

reunion ahead that should not fail to spill over into these journeying days, giving us joy.

Two travellers were walking together on a journey. You
could tell that they were not happy by the way they walked –
heads down, hardly aware of the road they were travelling.
Their hopes had been crushed and they were left deeply disappointed, possibly heading for home. Quitting. We all know
what that feels like because life is often like that – unpredicta-
ble. Then someone came alongside them and, taking an interest in them, asked why they were so downcast. They replied
with words that you and I have probably often used ourselves:
'We had hoped . . .' I am sure that you recognize the story of
the disciples on the road to Emmaus, found in Luke 24:13–35.
They had begun to put their trust in Jesus, believing him to be
the promised one, the answer to their hopes, but he had been
crucified and their hopes had died with him.

Many of us can probably identify with that story, knowing
what it is like to look to the Lord for something, albeit help
in a difficult situation, healing for a loved one, restored harmony in a relationship – only to be disappointed. We wonder
where the Lord was because he seems to have withdrawn his
presence, leaving us disappointed. 'We had hoped . . .' But this
story graphically tells us that we do not have to stay in that
state; in fact, I would go as far as to say that God's intention
for us is that we should not remain in that state of sadness and
discouragement. When our daughter died we were, of course,
heart-broken and deeply disappointed that our prayers did not
result in her being healed. We tussled in our thinking, trying to
understand and come to terms with what had happened. But,
I am pleased to say, our heavenly Father did not leave us there!
We have not become sad, disappointed people who no longer
know how to laugh, because that is not his intention or purpose

for our lives. Whatever you may think, it is not a sign of great spirituality to look perpetually serious, complete with furrowed brow and absence of a sense of humour. Such a lifestyle would be a poor witness to the one in whose presence there is 'fullness of joy' and at whose 'right hand are pleasures for evermore.'[2] Instead, true to his Word, we discovered that the Lord comes close to the broken-hearted, as we read in Psalm 34:18, just as he did to those disappointed disciples on the road to Emmaus.

When they finally realized that this was Jesus speaking with them, they said to each other those wonderful words: 'Were not our hearts burning within us while he talked with us . . .?'[3] It was as they fellowshipped with Jesus that their sadness lifted and their hearts were warmed. If you read the story, you will notice that it was actually in the intimacy of sharing food around a table that their eyes were opened to see Jesus. Such is the miracle of fellowship with Jesus, it is transformative. It is fellowshipping with Jesus that makes it possible to walk through the darkest circumstances of life without being crushed and robbed of our hope and joy.

So, what does it mean to fellowship with Jesus? What might that look like in the daily routines of our lives? Personally, I think that a daily practice of finding time alone with the Lord first thing in the morning is most helpful, to set one's compass and listen to the most important voice before all the noise of the day begins. There are so many voices competing for our attention on a moment-by-moment basis, be it social media posts or news headlines, and it is all too easy for our thinking and our emotions to be seduced or drawn in, often in unhelpful ways. I am something of a morning person, enjoying the early hours of the day, and I realize that others think of themselves as night owls, coming alive later on, but it would seem that the psalmist agreed with me: 'Awake, my glory! Awake, harp and lyre! I will awake the dawn! I will give thanks to you, O Lord, among the peoples; I will sing praises to you among the nations.'[4] Like the psalmist, let there be singing, praising and giving thanks!

As I mentioned earlier, we often speak about having 'quiet times' or devotionals, which I have to say more often than not brings back images of rather sober early morning moments sitting alone, trying very hard to concentrate, to read the Bible and pray without allowing myself to be distracted by the multitude of alternative options that presented themselves. Fortunately, our fellowship with Jesus does not have to be like that! I actually rather like the word 'devotion' because it is important that our devotion to Jesus is at the heart of our fellowshipping with him in prayer and the Word, but I happily ignore the idea of having 'quiet times', because it is most often the case that it is preferable if they are not quiet!

In this book, I have written about the importance of singing in our devotion to Jesus, and how the Holy Spirit can and does help us. I have mentioned J.I. Packer's description of what the Holy Spirit does in our lives, likening it to floodlights – he turns on the floodlights so that we can see Jesus more clearly. I first read that illustration many years ago, shortly after returning from a visit to Barcelona. If you have ever been to that colourful place, you will know that it is famous for one of its former residents, Gaudi, whose creations are to be seen all over the city. Gaudi was an architect and designer whose work is, well, unusual to say the least, and quite stunning. One of the many inspirations for his work came from nature, so instead of straight lines, square doors and windows and smooth surfaces, his buildings with their tree-like curves and cave-like entrances would be more at home in a woodland than a high street. As well as designing buildings, he also designed sculptures, ceramics, lampposts, news stands, stained-glass windows and even a public park. But he is best remembered for the cathedral that he designed and oversaw the building of in Barcelona, the *La Sagrada Familia*. Angie and I went to see it one evening when daylight was fading, and our first impression on arriving was one of disappointment; it was just a large, grey building. But then the spotlights went on! Suddenly what had a moment before appeared to be dull and uninspiring was now breathtakingly striking. Instead of the usual tall, straight cathedral spires, these were all curved, and instead of evil-looking gargoyles, adorning the roof there were flying lions and wheat sheaves and colourful clusters of grapes – all now stunningly visible in the floodlights. What those spotlights did for that cathedral, the Holy Spirit does for our vision of Jesus and our understanding of Bible truth. He wants to turn the floodlights on Jesus, to open our eyes and expand our vision with the wonder of who he is, to warm our hearts and fill us with joy for the journey. That is why the apostle Paul prayed the way he did for Christians in Ephesus. He knew that at a time when they were facing growing persecution and when he himself was in jail under a sentence of death, they needed the help of the Holy Spirit to open their eyes and fill their hearts with the reality of wonderful, reassuring, rock-like future hope that was theirs in Christ:

> I keep asking that the God of our Lord Jesus Christ, the glorious Father, may give you the Spirit of wisdom and revelation, so that you may know him better. I pray that the eyes of your heart may be enlightened in order that you may know the hope to which he has called you, the riches of his glorious inheritance in his holy people . . .
>
> *Eph. 1:17–18*

Rather than praying for their circumstances to change, he prays for something of greater value and significance, something of eternal value. Of all the things he could have prayed for them, this is top of the list: he prayed they would know God better. Then he prays that the eyes of their hearts would be opened, that they would know their high calling, their future hope; not just in their minds, but in their hearts, their inner being, by the Spirit. As Christians we have a future, a wonderful, truly glorious future, a hope that is not in any doubt, and when our connection to that future becomes more than wishful thinking through the Holy Spirit's presence in our lives, then it radically changes us. The truth is we need the Holy Spirit's presence and help if we are to know and follow Jesus closely throughout our lives.

As well as floodlights, there is another analogy that J.I. Packer uses:

> The Spirit, we might say, is the matchmaker, the celestial marriage broker, whose role is to bring us and Christ together and ensure that we stay together.[5]

This is what the Holy Spirit seeks to do in our lives; to glorify Jesus and enrich our devotion to him, strengthening our desire to be with him face to face which, as we have already seen, is the heart of our future hope. He wants to give us not just a glimpse of our future inheritance, but also a foretaste, a taste before time. Why would we not invite the Holy Spirit to come flood our lives, just as he did those first Christians who we have read about in the New Testament, filling them with overflowing joy and courage for the journey? Why would we not each day give time and opportunity to allow the Holy Spirit to turn the floodlights on Jesus as we worship him, singing his praises, and thereby stay close to him? As pastor, speaker and writer R.T. Kendall says:

> I believe that every Christian has one fundamental calling and one primary duty – a duty which is also a delight. We are called, by the way we live and in all we do, to worship God. This is a full-time activity, not only here, but in heaven too.[6]

As well as being something very personal that we need to learn to foster in the hidden moments of our lives, fellowshipping with Jesus is also something that grows and flourishes in the company of other Christians. Look again at the story of those travellers on the road to Emmaus. What was their first reaction when their hearts were warmed by Jesus' presence? They had the energy to straight away run the seven miles or so, according to Luke 24:13, all the way back to Jerusalem to share the news with their friends! No doubt with considerable joy on the journey! See how Luke describes what happened shortly after they arrived back in Jerusalem and excitedly told their story to the other disciples. Jesus appeared once more and they were 'startled and frightened', so he invited them to touch his hands and feet and ate some food to make it clear to them that he was really alive and present with them. Luke tells us that they were struggling to understand it because of their 'joy and amazement'.[7] What had previously been a number of confused, disappointed individuals was becoming a company of friends who would shortly burst upon the world with the Good News that Jesus, the Saviour of the world was alive, present and active! The church was born.

Being part of a lively, committed local church family is not just part of the richness and joy of being a Christian; it is essential for our wellbeing, keeping us close to Jesus and maturing as Christians. The pages of the book of Acts are alive with the story of those first Jesus followers. We see them joyfully bursting out onto the streets of Jerusalem, testifying to the Good News of Jesus being alive. We see them devoted, not just to Jesus and the apostles' teachings but also to one another, in fellowship; opening their homes, eating, breaking bread, praying and praising God together daily. Luke, the author of Acts, tells us that they opened their lives to one another, making sure that no one was in need – what a beautiful community that must have been! Hardly surprisingly, people were 'added to their number daily'.[8] As the gospel spread from town to town new church families came into being, often in the face of severe opposition, but the church just grew and grew, to the point that they were accused of turning the world 'upside down'![9]

In encouraging those first churches, Paul often wrote in his letters reminders to them of their common calling as the body of Christ, interdependent and reliant on one another; or as God's temple, formed to be indwelt by the Holy Spirit. No wonder he so often urged them to be 'of one mind', to work hard to preserve their unity, and not to neglect their 'meeting together'[10] – such is the importance of Christian fellowship! But it is in what we might call the 'one-anothering' encouragements of the New Testament that we see the wonderful outworking of Christian fellowship, and how it can and should benefit and build us up as we each take our place and play our part. I will mention just a few: 'encourage one another and build each other up', 'serve one another humbly in love', 'Be kind and compassionate to one another', 'let us consider how we may spur one another on towards love and good deeds', 'love one another deeply, from the heart'.[11] What a wonderful context in which to live the Christian life!

Speaking personally, it has been one of the joys of my life that I have in my lifetime seen the emergence of new Spirit-filled churches and the restoration of many churches from sombre formalism to the Spirit-filled, life-giving example that we see in the book of Acts. For the past thirty years or more, Angie and I have been very much a part of the same church family here in Norwich, building deep and lasting relationships as we have fellowshipped, walking together almost on a daily basis, opening our hearts and homes to one another, talking, eating, praying, worshipping, weeping and laughing with people who have become good friends through the good times and the difficult times. The COVID-19 epidemic has made us aware just how precious this fellowship is – being together in the same room with our Christian brothers and sisters, singing our worship to the Lord, being together in all the ways mentioned above. It is truly life-giving and builds us up, giving us joy on the journey. And in our recent times of difficulty personally, our church family, this fellowship of friends, has been a wonderful source of love and support. Almost from the first day I was diagnosed with cancer, more than twelve years ago to the present day, a small group of friends have gathered together with Angie and myself to share our hearts and pray together (and often eat!) every few weeks. How precious is that – so encouraging!

As for when our daughter died, there are many stories I could tell of how the church family loved and supported us through that difficult time, but I will tell you of just one. It was a Sunday morning just days after it had happened, the first Sunday we had been back with our church, and Angie and I were mingling, almost wishing the meeting to begin so we could avoid conversation. Across the auditorium I noticed a tall guy making his way over towards us, a dear friend, Jon.

When he got to us he just embraced us in a bear hug, and simply said, 'We love you, guys,' and made his way back to his family. I can't tell you how much that meant. We couldn't cope with conversation – we were too raw – but how good it was to know the presence and love of our church family. It has been and continues to be a source of great encouragement, comfort and joy on the journey.

We are nearing the end of our brief study of the Christian's future hope. We have looked at how important it is for us as human beings to have things to look forward to, to hope for, and I have attempted to show how our future hope as Christians, properly grasped, not only enriches our lives, driving out our insecurities and fears, but equips us to walk through the darkest moments. It prevents us from being crushed by disappointments, distracted by fleeting worldly alternatives, and keeps us bonded to our Saviour while on our journey.

16

The Life You Always Wanted

The meals of Jesus are a sign of hope . . . It is hope for a renewed creation with bodies and food. It is hope for a meal, a meal in the presence of God. In the meantime, every meal is a picture of God's goodness and a reminder of his coming world.

Tim Chester[1]

One of my favourite pastimes is sitting around the table with family and friends to enjoy conversation and a good meal together. For me, it brings together many of the things that I value and enjoy most in life. I can imagine now the warmth of friendship, the good conversation, the laughter, playful humour, sharing of news and of course the tasty food, possibly accompanied with a glass of fine wine – perfect! We have a little tradition in our family of celebrating birthdays by gathering either at home or in a restaurant to enjoy a meal together; enjoying one another's company, thinking of the years past and catching up on latest family happenings, all the while laying down fond memories to be savoured for years to come. Such is the richness of life spent in community, in family, in relationships, without which life becomes more like existing than living. Everyone knows that solitary confinement is a form of punishment, and although some of us probably quite like our own company from time to time, the fact is we are social creatures, and life without the interaction of others quickly becomes tedious. Two years of COVID-19 taught us that. Oh, how we longed to be in the same room with friends and loved ones, especially those living alone, to be free of masks, hugging instead of bumping elbows, smiling and maybe even offering a kiss!

Our bodies matter because they express something of who we are and not just in our looks, important though they are. The wonderful variety and giftedness of human beings is mediated through the expressions on our faces, our laughter (be it raucous or subdued), our ability to sing (or not), to run, dance, play sport or a musical instrument, and we can even express approval or disapproval, compassion or anger with the smallest gesture without even uttering a word. Then of course there is touch, embrace, the squeeze of a hand – how important that is and how appreciated in tender or painful moments. This is what makes us fully human, as is quickly recognized when those movements and responses are taken away either through illness, accident or ageing. It is a great sadness to see friends who were once active and agile suddenly become straightjacketed, perhaps through injury or a debilitating illness, and become something less than they used to be. And then there is death, when everything goes silent and stops.

I am so glad that Jesus rose from the grave physically. I am so glad that he took time to be with his disciples, to show them that he was not a ghost or just a spirit. They took some persuading! After urging them to touch him to prove that he really did have real flesh and bones, as a last resort he asked for some fish so as to prove that he could eat too. Look at Luke's account:

> [']Look at my hands and my feet. It is I myself! Touch me and see; a ghost does not have flesh and bones, as you see I have.' When he

had said this, he showed them his hands and feet. And while they still did not believe it because of joy and amazement, he asked them, 'Do you have anything here to eat?' They gave him a piece of broiled fish, and he took it and ate it in their presence.

Luke 24:39–40

Why am I making so much of this? Why is it so important? Because this shows us that the great hope of the Christian really does win. If our future destiny is just to float around nebulously in some spirit world, then it would not be true to say that death has been defeated because such an existence would be less than human life in all its fullness, whereas the Bible tells us otherwise. Do you know what will happen at the culmination of time when sin has been dealt with, wrongdoings judged and death destroyed? The redeemed – that's you and me, if you are a Christian – will be invited to a dinner party, a banquet, and not any old dinner party. We are back to the subject of one of my favourite pastimes! To the shout of multiple angelic hallelujahs we will be invited to a marriage feast to celebrate the marriage of the Lamb, King Jesus, to his bride, the church, who, united at last, will enjoy his new creation together for eternity. There will be singing and glad exchanges because we will have smiles and ears and mouths and vocal cords that work rather better than the ones we have at present. And as well as unimaginable delicacies, there will be wine! You may remember that during the Last Supper Jesus told his disciples that he would not drink of the fruit of the vine until he drank it again in his Father's kingdom.[2] Then, in the conclusion of the book of Revelation, John looks and sees the new heaven and new earth, the first heaven and earth with its death, mourning and pain having passed away, and he hears God speak personally and directly to declare that he is making everything new. The unblemished beauty of Eden is restored, with no curse, and the undiminished enjoyment of God's presence and creation is to be enjoyed forever.

Let me now apply all that I have just said to the subject of our hope. In the quotation at the start of this chapter, pastor and author Tim Chester rightly says: 'The meals of Jesus are a sign of hope . . . It is hope for a renewed creation with bodies and food. It is hope for a meal, a meal in the presence of God.' You might think that it sounds rather frivolous to suggest that God should have an interest is something as ordinary and human as a meal, but it really isn't. Actually, as author Mike Breen comments in his endorsement in the book *A Meal with Jesus*: '. . . if you take mountains and meals out of the Bible, it is a very short book!'[3] The point he is making is that God prizes the beauty of his creation and puts a high value on human relationships. The trouble is that we have so bought in to the Ancient Greek concept of matter – of bodies and what we do with them as being rather mundane and grubby, whereas things of the spirit realm are considered to be superior and pure – that we are in danger of losing sight of what the Bible teaches. When God created the heavens and the earth, he repeatedly declared it to be good. It is true that as a result of humanity's rebellion it now bears a curse,[4] but come the new creation when all is purified,[5] restored and untainted by curse, it will bear the hallmarks and beauty of the first creation. It will not be obliterated; rather, it will be made new, made more glorious. Jesus' death and resurrection accomplished more than the forgiveness of our sins, wonderful though that is. It set in motion God's plan to restore all things, including the whole cosmos. In his letter to believers in Colossae, Paul writes about the supremacy of the now risen, ascended Lord Jesus, how all of creation came into being through him and for him. He goes on to say that God's plan

in sending his Son was 'through him to reconcile to himself all
things, whether things on earth or things in heaven, by making
peace through his blood, shed on the cross'.[6] What a wonderful future! What a beautiful prospect, not just us his redeemed
people but all of creation in harmony again with its creator.
Writing to Christians in Rome, Paul expresses his own longing
for this new day and tells us that, in some way, all of creation is
groaning like a pregnant woman longing to give birth.[7]

What does this mean for us? It means that in the final analysis, on the Last Day, when Jesus returns in great glory to bring
judgement and right wrongs, to raise the dead and make all
things new, we will be caught up to meet him in the air, face
to face at last.[8] Death will truly be undone and we will live –
really live – the lives we always wanted! Complete with bodies
and a beautiful creation we will have uninterrupted enjoyment
of our Lord and Saviour's presence. Ours is not a future float-
ing around on clouds. Rather it is an eternity living with new
bodies that will not age, malfunction or get sick, able to do and
enjoy pleasures that we only ever dreamed of (such as playing
the saxophone, I like to think!) in the company of those we
love and have possibly been parted from, while cherishing a
face-to-face relationship with our Lord and Saviour. Home at
last, hope having won. I mention being in the presence of those
we love and have been parted from, and that is for many of us
a wonderful thought. As Christians, we will be reunited, with
no cancer, no deformity, no sadness – just the joy of reunion,
of smile, of touch, of embrace that will far outshine the fondest
memory.

One of the dangers of bereavement and of getting old for
that matter, is nostalgia. It can be all too easy to live in the past,
wishing that bygone days were still here, daydreaming or possibly even mourning happier days when you were young, fit,

attractive or perhaps when that loved one was still alive. This is not to be the way of the Christian. Memories can certainly be very precious and as such should be treasured with gratitude, but when they cause us to be sorrowful and even despairing it is a sure sign that we lack the future hope that God intends us to have. We are looking in the wrong direction and are in danger of being robbed of our joy. You have probably heard of the famous mile race between Roger Bannister and John Landy. It became known as the 'Miracle Mile' because both Bannister and Landy were the only runners in the world who had run the mile in less than four minutes. In that much-publicized race in Vancouver in 1954, John Landy was in the lead entering the last lap and looked to be on his way to a famous victory. But on the last bend he failed to hear Bannister, now on his shoulder, turned to look behind him and at that very moment Bannister overtook him on his blind side, and won the race.

If we were clearer and more confident about the certainty of that future hope, of the restoration and enjoyment of everything that God has in store for us, then we would discover that rather than reminiscing unhelpfully and living with regret and sadness, our lives become happily energized with the prospect of what is ahead. It can warm our hearts and quicken our pace as we run with all our energy to obtain it. The apostle Paul encourages us to have the same attitude towards our future as the runner out to win gold. Writing to Christians in Philippi who were facing similar struggles to his own,[9] he urges them to have the same perspective as his: 'Brothers and sisters, I do not consider myself yet to have taken hold of it. But one thing I do: forgetting what is behind and straining towards what is ahead, I press on towards the goal to win the prize for which God has called me heavenwards in Christ Jesus. All of us, then, who are mature should take such a view of things.'[10]

'Forgetting what is behind and straining towards what is ahead' is a graphic expression reflecting the utter commitment, intent and priority of a runner determined to give their all to get to that finishing line to win. What is this forgetting of the past which Paul urges with such emphasis? It is the sort of dwelling on the past that hinders us in the present. We do well to remind ourselves gently that a bereavement can sometimes cause us to live in the past, possibly regretting things that we said or did, or grieving things we left unsaid or undone. Similarly, it is all too easy to harbour ongoing bitterness about past wrongs (real or supposed). There are few things that have such power as regret or bitterness to lock us unhelpfully into the past. Then there is despair over past sins and failings which, in its severest form, can make us doubt if we will ever be forgiven. Paul will have none of it! No nostalgic looking back. Not a hint of settledness, complacency or uncertainty, but instead a passionate longing for the prize and his enjoyment of it. Of course, one needs to ask what that prize was for Paul and what can it be for us. You have read the answer several times already on previous pages but I will allow Paul to tell us in his own words. As well as the joy of reunions and the beauty of heaven, it is a prize that is able to capture all your affections and then never fade but only become increasingly wonderful.

> I consider everything a loss because of the surpassing worth of knowing Christ Jesus my Lord, for whose sake I have lost all things. I consider them garbage, that I may gain Christ . . . I want to know Christ – yes, to know the power of his resurrection and participation in his sufferings, becoming like him in his death, and so, somehow, attaining to the resurrection from the dead.
>
> *Phil. 3:8–11*

For Paul, the greatest reward was to know Christ fully and to experience perfect fellowship with him, face to face. This is the prize that Paul wanted his readers and us to have our eyes fixed on. A hope that wins.

There is a wonderful moment at the climax of the Chronicles of Narnia when the children are just beginning to enjoy the new Narnia, but are nervous that it may not last. Aslan, the Christ figure, seeing this, reassures them:

> Then Aslan turned to them and said: 'You do not yet look so happy as I mean you to be.' Lucy said, 'We are so afraid of being sent away, Aslan. And you have sent us back into our own world so often.' 'No fear of that,' said Aslan. 'Have you not guessed?' Their hearts leaped and a wild hope rose within them. 'There was a real railway accident,' said Aslan softly. 'Your father and mother and all of you are – as you used to call it in the Shadowlands – dead. The term is over: the holidays have begun. The dream is ended: this is the morning.'[11]

Bibliography

Ash, Christopher. *Job: The Wisdom of the Cross* (Wheaton, IL: Crossway, Good News Publishers, 2014).

Bernard of Cluny. *The Celestial Country*, 12th century. Translated from Latin to English by John Mason Neale 1865. Reworked by Dan Jones, *The Land For Which We Long*, 2021. Not yet published.

Bonhoeffer, Dietrich. *Life Together* (London: SCM Press Ltd, 2005).

Bunyan, John. *The Pilgrim's Progress* (Grand Rapids, MI: Zondervan, 1976).

Carmichael, Amy. *A Very Present Help* (Ann Arbor, MI: Servant Books, 1996).

Carson, D.A. *How Long, O Lord?* (Nottingham: IVP, 2006).

Chester, Tim. *A Meal with Jesus* (Nottingham: IVP, 2011).

Eaton, Michael. *How to Enjoy God's Worldwide Church* (Tonbridge: Sovereign World Ltd, 1995).

Frankl, Viktor. *Man's Search for Meaning* (New York: Penguin Random House; Ebury Digital, 2013).

Giglio, Louie and Matt Redman. *Indescribable* (Colorado Springs: David C. Cook, 2011).

Grudem, Wayne. *1 Peter* (Tyndale New Testament Commentaries) (Leicester: IVP, 1989).

Guthrie, Nancy. *Be Still, My Soul* (London: IVP, 2010).

Keller, Timothy. *On Death* (London: Hodder & Stoughton, 2020).

Kendall, R.T. *Worshipping God* (Lady Mary, FL: Charisma House, 2017).

King, Martin Luther. *Strength to Love* (Glasgow: Fontana Books, 1970).

King, Martin Luther. *The Trumpet of Conscience* (London: Harper-Collins, 1989).

Lewis, C.S. *A Grief Observed* (London: Faber & Faber, 2013).

Lewis, C.S. *Mere Christianity* (Glasgow: Fontana Books, 1956).

Lewis, C.S. *The Last Battle* (Glasgow: William Collins Sons & Co., 1981).

Lewis, C.S. *The Magician's Nephew* (Glasgow: Fontana Lions, 1981).

Lewis, C.S. *The Problem of Pain* (London: Fount Paperbacks, 1978).

Lewis, C.S. *The Weight of Glory* (New York: Touchstone Books, 1996).

Lloyd-Jones, Martyn. *Joy Unspeakable* (Sussex: David C. Cook, Kingsway Communications Ltd., 2008).

Lloyd-Jones, Martyn. *Romans: Exposition of Chapter 8:5–17* (Edinburgh: Banner of Truth Trust, 1974).

Lloyd-Jones, Martyn. *The Unsearchable Riches of Christ: An Exposition of Ephesians 3* (Edinburgh: Banner of Truth Trust, 1979).

Luther, Martin. *A Commentary on St Paul's Epistle to the Galatians* (trans. Theodore Graebner; Grand Rapids, MI: Zondervan, 1949).

Luther, Martin. *Luther's Works: Lectures on Isaiah Chapter 40–66* (trans: H.J.A. Bouman; St Louis, MO: Concordia Publishing House, 1972).

Moo, Douglas J. *The Epistle to the Romans* (Grand Rapids, MI: Eerdmans, 1996).

Nouwen, Henri J.M. *In the House of the Lord* (London: Darton, Longman & Todd, 1986).

Packer, J.I. *Keep in Step with the Spirit* (London: IVP, 2001).

Packer, J.I. *Knowing God* (London: Hodder & Stoughton, 1973).

Packer, J.I. *Laid-back Religion?* (Nottingham: IVP, 1989).

Packer, J.I. 'Our Lifeline', *Christianity Today*, 28 Oct. 1996, https://www.christianitytoday.com/ct/1996/october28/6tc022.html (accessed 11 Nov. 2022).

Packer, J.I. *Weakness is the Way* (Wheaton, IL: Crossway, Good News Publishers, 2014).

Peterson, Eugene. *A Long Obedience in the Same Direction* (Downers Grove, IL: IVP, 2000).

Phillips, J.B. *The New Testament in Modern English* (Glasgow: Collins Font Paperbacks, 1960, 1972).

Piper, John. 'Living Supernaturally as the Church of Christ', *Desiring God*, 30 Sept. 1992, https://www.desiringgod.org/articles/living-supernaturally-as-the-church-of-christ (accessed 7 Nov. 2022).

Piper, John. 'The Cosmic Church', *Desiring God*, 22 Mar. 1981, https://www.desiringgod.org/messages/the-cosmic-church (accessed 10 Nov. 2022).

Poythress, Vern. *The Returning King* (Phillipsburg, NJ: P&R Publishing, 2000).

Sargent, Tony. *Gems from Martyn Lloyd-Jones* (Milton Keynes: Authentic Media, 2007).

Tolkien, J.R.R. *The Lord of the Rings* (London: HarperCollins, 2007).

Virgo, Terry. *A People Prepared* (Eastbourne: Kingsway Publications, 1996).

Vroegop, Mark. *Dark Clouds, Deep Mercy* (Wheaton, IL: Crossway, Good News Publishers, 2019).

Music

Green, Melody. 'There Is A Redeemer', CMG Song no. 3018. © 1982 Birdwing Music (ASCAP), Ears to Hear Music (ASCAP), Universal Music – Brentwood Benson Publ. (ASCAP) (adm. at CapitolCMPPublishing.com).

Knight, Olly and James Palmer, 'God of all Comfort', CCLI 7037762, 2015, from *The Stream*, published by PushMusic Publishing, www.worshipJesus.co.uk.

Knight, Olly, Tim Mann, Phil Moore and Josh Rayner, 'Longing', CCLI 7155379, 2020, from *You Hold the World*, www.worshipJesus.co.uk.

Newton, John. (1725–1807) 'Amazing Grace', lyrics found on https://gccsatx.com/hymns/amazing-grace/ (accessed 8 Jul. 2022).

Redman, Matt, Beth Redman and Leonard Jarman, 'One Day (When We All Get To Heaven)', CMG Song no. 119574 © 2017 Thankyou Music (PRS) (adm. worldwide at CapitolCMGPublishing.com excluding the UK & Europe which is adm. at Integrated Rights.com) / worshiptogether.com, Songs (ASCAP), sixsteps Music (ASCAP), Said And Done Music (ASCAP) (adm. at CapitolCMGPublishing.com).

Redman, Matt. 'The Father's Song', CMG Song no. 26466. Copyright © 2000 Thankyou Music (PRS) (adm. worldwide at CapitolCMGPublishing.com excluding the UK & Europe which is adm. at IntegratedRights.com).

Story, Laura. 'Blessings', CMG Song no. 65638. Copyright © 2011 Laura Stories (ASCAP), New Spring Publishing Inc. (ASCAP) (adm. at CapitolCMGPublishing.com).

Notes

Introduction

[1] Taken from *Job: The Wisdom of the Cross*, by Christopher Ash, © 2014, p. 18. Used by permission of Crossway, a publishing ministry of Good News Publishers, Wheaton, IL 60187, www.crossway.org.

[2] 1 Pet. 1:8.

1. Hope on Trial

[1] Acts 1:5.

[2] J.I. Packer, *Keep in Step with the Spirit* (London: IVP, 2001), p. 65.

[3] 2 Sam. 23:1, NET.

2. When Hope Dies

[1] Martin Luther King, *The Trumpet of Conscience* (London: Harper-Collins, 1989). Reprinted by arrangement with The Heirs to the Estate of Martin Luther King Jr., c/o Writers House as agent for the proprietor New York, NY. Copyright © 1963 by Dr. Martin Luther King, Jr. Renewed © 1992 by Coretta Scott King.

2 Denis Campbell, *The Guardian*, 'NHS prescribed record number of antidepressants last year', 29 Jun. 2017, https://www.theguardian .com/society/2017/jun/29/nhs-prescribed-record-number-of-antidepressants-last-year (accessed 4 October 2022).

3 Linda Pressly, BBC News, 'Resignation Syndrome: Sweden's mystery illness', 26 Oct. 2017, https://www.bbc.co.uk/news/ magazine-41748485 (accessed 3 August 2022).

4 Viktor Frankl, *Man's Search for Meaning* (New York: Penguin Random House; Ebury Digital, 2013), Kindle edition, location 1020.

5 Gen. 1:27.

6 Martin Luther King, *Strength to Love* (Glasgow: Fontana Books, 1970), p. 95. Reprinted by arrangement with The Heirs to the Estate of Martin Luther King Jr., c/o Writers House as agent for the proprietor New York, NY. Copyright © 1963 by Dr. Martin Luther King, Jr. Renewed © 1992 by Coretta Scott King.

3. Hope in the Face of Illness

1 C.S. Lewis, *The Problem of Pain* (London: Fount Paperbacks, 1978), p. 81. Copyright © 1940 C.S. Lewis Pte. Ltd. Extract reprinted by permission.

2 Gen. 1:27.

3 2 Cor. 4:16.

4 Henri J.M. Nouwen, *In the House of the Lord* (London: Darton, Longman & Todd, 1986), p. 7. Reprinted by permission.

5 Nouwen, *In the House of the Lord*, pp. 4–5. Reprinted by permission.

6 J.I. Packer, 'Our Lifeline', *Christianity Today*, 28 Oct. 1996, https://www.christianitytoday.com/ct/1996/october28/6tc022. html (accessed 11 Nov. 2022).

7 Nancy Guthrie, *Be Still, My Soul* (London: IVP, 2010), p. 33. Reproduced by kind permission.

8 Dietrich Bonhoeffer, *Life Together* (London: SCM Press Ltd, 2005), pp. 27ff. Reproduced by kind permission.

9 J.I. Packer, *Knowing God* (London: Hodder & Stoughton, 1973), p. 37.

4. Hope in the Face of a Father

[1] Martin Luther, *A Commentary on St Paul's Epistle to the Galatians* (trans. Theodore Graebner; Grand Rapids, MI: Zondervan, 2nd edn; 1st edn 1949).

[2] Matt Redman, 'The Father's Song', CMG Song no. 26466. Copyright © 2000 Thankyou Music (PRS) (adm. worldwide at CapitolCMGPublishing.com excluding the UK & Europe which is adm. at IntegratedRights.com). All rights reserved. Used by permission.

[3] Eph. 1:6, KJV.

[4] J.I. Packer, *Knowing God* (London: Hodder & Stoughton, 1973), p. 182.

[5] Eph. 2:12.

[6] 1 John 3:1.

[7] Douglas J. Moo, *The Epistle to the Romans* (Grand Rapids, MI: Eerdmans, 1996), pp. 499, 502. Reproduced with kind permission.

[8] Dr Martyn Lloyd-Jones, *Romans: Exposition of Chapter 8:5–17* (Edinburgh: Banner of Truth Trust, 1974), pp. 272f, 284. Reproduced with kind permission.

[9] See John 14:18.

[10] John 14:17.

[11] 2 Cor. 12:9.

5. Finding Hope in Hard Places

[1] Laura Story, 'Blessings', CMG Song no. 65638. Copyright © 2011 Laura Stories (ASCAP) New Spring Publishing Inc. (ASCAP) (adm. at CapitolCMGPublishing.com). All rights reserved. Used by permission.

[2] John Bunyan, *The Pilgrim's Progress* (Grand Rapids, MI: Zondervan, 1976), p. 20.

[3] 2 Cor. 12:9.

4   Taken from *Weakness is the Way* by J.I. Packer © 2014, p. 116.
    Used by permission of Crossway, a publishing ministry of Good
    News Publishers, Wheaton, IL 60187, www.crossway.org.
5   John Newton (1725–1807), 'Amazing Grace', lyrics found on
    https://gccsatx.com/hymns/amazing-grace/ (accessed 8 Jul. 2022).
6   Laura Story, 'Blessings', CMG Song no. 65638. Copyright
    © 2011 Laura Stories (ASCAP) New Spring Publishing Inc.
    (ASCAP) (adm. at CapitolCMGPublishing.com). All rights re-
    served. Used by permission.

6. Hope in the Face of Death

1   Timothy Keller, *On Death* (London: Hodder & Stoughton,
    2020), pp. 1–2.
2   Generally attributed to Benjamin Franklin.
3   Graham Tomlin, *The Times*, www.thetimes.co.uk/article/its-far-
    too-late-to-think-about-death-when-youre-dying-lets-do-it-now-
    3ns35mwfb (accessed 8 July 2022).
4   Melody Green, 'There Is A Redeemer', CMG Song no. 3018.
    © 1982 Birdwing Music (ASCAP) Ears to Hear Music (ASCAP)
    Universal Music – Brentwood Benson Publ. (ASCAP) (adm.
    at CapitolCMPPublishing.com). All rights reserved. Used by
    permission.
5   See John 11.
6   For example, 1 Cor. 1:8.
7   See also 2 Thess. 1:7–10; 2 Pet. 3; Rev. 21.
8   C.S. Lewis, *A Grief Observed* (London: Faber & Faber, 2013),
    pp. 45–46. © 1961 C.S. Lewis Pte. Ltd. Extract reprinted by
    permission.
9   Ps. 90:10, KJV.
10 Martyn Lloyd-Jones, *Banner of Truth*, Issue 275. Quoted in Tony
    Sargent, *Gems from Martyn Lloyd-Jones* (Milton Keynes: Authen-
    tic Media, 2007), p. 84.
11 Matthew 16:24–27; John 3:16–21.

12 Martin Luther, *Luther's Works: Lectures on Isaiah Chapter 40–66* (trans: H.J.A. Bouman; St Louis, MO: Concordia Publishing House, 1972), pp. 223f.

13 1 Cor. 15:17ff; 1 Thess. 4:14.

14 Luke 23:43.

15 John 14:1–4.

7. Why, O Lord?

1 Taken from *Dark Clouds, Deep Mercy*, by Mark Vroegop, © 2019, p. 26. Used by permission of Crossway, a publishing ministry of Good News Publishers, Wheaton, IL 60187, www.crossway.org.

2 Job 16:2.

3 Taken from *Job: The Wisdom of the Cross*, by Christopher Ash, © 2014, p. 429. Used by permission of Crossway, a publishing ministry of Good News Publishers, Wheaton, IL 60187, www. crossway.org.

8. Rediscovering Heaven

1 J.R.R. Tolkien, *The Lord of the Rings* (London: HarperCollins, 2007 Edition), p. 951. Reprinted by permission of HarperCollins Publishers Ltd © 1955, J.R.R. Tolkien.

2 See Isa. 51:3; Ezek. 28:13; 31:8.

3 Bunyan, *The Pilgrim's Progress* (Michigan: Zondervan, 1967), pp. 286, 25.

4 Eugene Peterson, *A Long Obedience in the Same Direction* (Downers Grove, IL: IVP, 2000), p. 17. Reproduced by kind permission.

5 Eph. 2:6; 2 Cor. 5:8; Matt. 6:19–20.

6 C.S. Lewis, *Mere Christianity* (Glasgow: Fontana Books, 1956), p. 116. Copyright © 1942, 1943, 1944, 1952 C.S. Lewis Pte. Ltd. Extract reprinted by permission.

[7] J.I. Packer, *Laid-back Religion?* (Nottingham: IVP, 1989), p. 63. © J.I. Packer 1987. Reproduced with permission of the licensor through PLSclear.

[8] For example, Matt. 4:19.

[9] Matt. 6:19.

[10] 1 Cor. 7:31.

[11] 1 John 2:15.

[12] 1 John 2:16.

[13] 1 Cor. 9:24.

[14] Phil. 3:12–14.

[15] Heb. 12:1–2.

9. Hope in an Uncertain World

[1] Bernard of Cluny, *The Celestial Country*, 12th century. Translated from Latin to English by John Mason Neale 1865. Reworked by Dan Jones, *The Land For Which We Long*, 2021. Not yet published, permission given.

[2] C.S. Lewis, *Mere Christianity* (Glasgow: Fontana Books, 1956), p. 116. Copyright © 1942, 1943, 1944, 1953 C.S. Lewis Pte. Ltd. Extract reprinted by permission.

[3] C.S. Lewis, *The Weight of Glory* (New York: Touchstone Books, 1996), pp. 36–37. Copyright © 1949 C.S. Lewis Pte Ltd. Extract reprinted by permission.

[4] Gen. 1:27.

[5] John 14:6.

[6] Michael Eaton, *How to Enjoy God's Worldwide Church* (Tonbridge: Sovereign World Ltd, 1995), p. 13. Reproduced by kind permission.

[7] Eaton, *How to Enjoy God's Worldwide Church*, p. 27.

[8] Rev. 21:5.

[9] Matt. 25:13, ESV.

[10] Ray Loynd, 'Charles Dutton Not a Prisoner of His Past', *Los Angeles Times*, 18 Jan. 1990, www.latimes.com (accessed 8 August 2022).

[11] Rewritten by Dan Jones, permission given.

10. Face to Face

1 Matt Redman, Beth Redman and Leonard Jarman, 'One Day (When We All Get To Heaven)', CMG Song no. 119574 © 2017 Thankyou Music (PRS) (adm. worldwide at Capitol-CMGPublishing.com excluding the UK & Europe which is adm. at IntegratedRights.com) / worshiptogether.com Songs (ASCAP) sixsteps Music (ASCAP) Said And Done Music (ASCAP) (adm. at CapitolCMGPublishing.com). All rights reserved. Used by permission.
2 Gen. 1:28.
3 Gen. 3:8.
4 Exod. 33:11.
5 Isa. 54:8.
6 Matt. 26:67, NASB95.
7 John 1:14.
8 2 Cor. 4:6.
9 Mark 9:2–12.
10 Mark 8:29.
11 Matt. 1:23.
12 See Phil. 2:6–9.
13 Charles Wesley (1707–78), 'Hark! The Herald Angels Sing', www.hymnal.net/en/hymn/h/84 (accessed 8 July 2022).
14 Matt. 27:51.
15 John 14:26, KJV.
16 Olly Knight, Tim Mann, Phil Moore and Josh Rayner, 'Longing', CCLI 7155379, 2020, from *You Hold the World*, www.worshipJesus.co.uk. Reproduced by kind permission.

11. Hope in the Face of Suffering

1 Nancy Guthrie, *Be Still, My Soul* (London: IVP, 2010), p. 33.
2 Job 30:20, ESV.
3 Job 42:5.
4 2 Cor. 12:7.

[5] Jas 5:14.

[6] 2 Cor. 4:17, ESV.

[7] D.A. Carson, *How Long, O Lord?* (Nottingham: IVP, 2006), p. 189. Reproduced by kind permission.

[8] Rom. 8:28.

[9] J.R.R. Tolkien, *The Lord of the Rings* (London: HarperCollins, 2007 Edition), p. 951. Reprinted by permission of HarperCollins Publishers Ltd © 1955, J.R.R. Tolkien.

[10] Heb. 12:2.

[11] See Rev. 21:4–5.

[12] Luke 22:33.

[13] Luke 22:54–62.

[14] John 21.

[15] Martyn Lloyd-Jones, *The Unsearchable Riches of Christ: An Exposition of Ephesians 3* (Edinburgh: Banner of Truth Trust, 1979), p. 119. Reproduced by kind permission.

[16] 1 Cor. 6:19.

[17] John Piper, 'Living Supernaturally as the Church of Christ', *Desiring God*, 30 Sept 1992, https://www.desiringgod.org/articles/living-supernaturally-as-the-church-of-christ (accessed 7 Nov. 2022). Reproduced by kind permission.

[18] Olly Knight and James Palmer, 'God of all Comfort', CCLI 7037762, 2015, from *The Stream*, published by PushMusic Publishing, www.worshipJesus.co.uk. Reproduced by kind permission.

12. Holding On to Hope

[1] 2 Cor. 1:8, ESV.

[2] 2 Cor. 12:9.

[3] Matt. 9:36.

[4] 1 Pet. 2:9.

[5] Titus 2:14.

[6] Rev. 22:17.

[7] Acts 2:42.

[8] Acts 2:46.

9 Acts 20:7.
10 Eph. 4:3.
11 Church, *ekklesia*, literally means 'called-out ones'.

13. Hope That Transforms Life

1 Martyn Lloyd-Jones, *Joy Unspeakable* (Sussex: David C. Cook, Kingsway Communications Ltd., 2008), p. 41. © 1984. Used by permission of David C. Cook. May not be further reproduced. All rights reserved.
2 Acts 16:25; Acts 5:40–41; Acts 12:2.
3 Acts 16:25.
4 Acts 6.
5 My emphasis.
6 J.B. Phillips, *The New Testament in Modern English* (Glasgow: Collins Font Paperbacks, 1960, 1972), p. 487.
7 Wayne Grudem, *1 Peter* (Tyndale New Testament Commentaries) (Leicester: IVP, 1989), p. 66. Reproduced by kind permission.
8 Neh. 8:10.
9 1 Chr. 15:16; 2 Chr. 5:13.
10 Ps. 98:7–8, ESV.
11 Job 38:7.
12 Rom. 8:19–22.
13 C.S. Lewis, *The Magician's Nephew* (Glasgow: Fontana Lions, 1981), p. 93. Copyright © 1955 C.S. Lewis Pte Ltd. Extract reprinted by permission.
14 John 14:18; John 14:16, KJV; John 14:17.
15 John 16:14.
16 1 Pet. 1:8.
17 1 Pet. 1:1, KJV.
18 Martyn Lloyd-Jones, *Joy Unspeakable* (Sussex: David C. Cook, Kingsway Communications Ltd., 2008), p. 46. © 1984. Used by permission of David C. Cook. May not be further reproduced. All rights reserved.
19 John 14:16, KJV, my emphasis.

[20] John 16:7, ESV.
[21] Acts 8; Acts 10; Acts 19:1–20.
[22] 1 Pet. 1:4.

14. Living Life with Heaven's Perspective

[1] Reprinted from *The Returning King* by Vern Poythress. Copyright 2000, P&R Publishing, Phillipsburg, NJ.
[2] Heb. 1:3.
[3] Louie Giglio and Matt Redman, *Indescribable* (Colorado Springs: David C. Cook, 2011), p. 200. © 2011. Used by permission of David C. Cook. May not be further reproduced. All rights reserved.
[4] Gen. 1:1.
[5] Terry Virgo, *A People Prepared* (Eastbourne: Kingsway Publications, 1996), p. 45.
[6] My emphasis.
[7] Rev. 21:5.
[8] 1 Cor. 15:35–43.
[9] Gen. 1:31.
[10] Gen. 1:28.
[11] John Piper, 'The Cosmic Church', *Desiring God*, 22 Mar. 1981, https://www.desiringgod.org/messages/the-cosmic-church (accessed 10 Nov. 2022). Reproduced by kind permission.

15. Joy on the Journey

[1] Amy Carmichael, *A Very Present Help* (Ann Arbor, MI: Servant Books, 1996), p. 60.
[2] Ps. 16:11, ESV.
[3] Luke 24:32.
[4] Ps. 57:8–9, ESV.
[5] J.I. Packer, *Keep in Step with the Spirit* (London: IVP, 2001), p. 65.

6   R.T. Kendall, *Worshipping God* (Lady Mary, FL: Charisma House, 2017), p. 1.
7   Luke 24:37,41.
8   Acts 2:42–47.
9   Acts 17:6, ESV.
10 Phil. 2:2; Eph. 4:3; Heb. 10:24.
11 1 Thess. 5:11; Gal. 5:13; Eph. 4:32; Heb. 10:24; 1 Pet. 1:22.

16. The Life You Always Wanted

1   Tim Chester, *A Meal with Jesus* (Nottingham: IVP, 2011), p. 78. Reproduced by kind permission.
2   Matt. 26:29.
3   Chester, *A Meal with Jesus*, opening page (not numbered). Reproduced by kind permission.
4   Gen. 3:17.
5   2 Pet. 3:7.
6   Col. 1:20.
7   Rom. 8:22–23.
8   1 Thess. 4:16–17.
9   Phil. 1:29–30.
10 Phil. 3:13–15.
11 C.S. Lewis, *The Last Battle* (Glasgow: William Collins Sons & Co., 1981), p. 172. Copyright © 1956 C.S. Lewis Pte Ltd. Extract reprinted by permission.

Authentic

We trust you enjoyed reading this book from Authentic. If you want to be informed of any new titles from this author and other releases you can sign up to the Authentic newsletter by scanning below:

Online:
authenticmedia.co.uk

Follow us: